# Crime and its treatment

## John Barron Mays, M.A., Ph.D.
Eleanor Rathbone Professor of Sociology
University of Liverpool

Longman

**LONGMAN GROUP LIMITED**
London
*Associated companies, branches and representatives throughout the world*

© *Longman Group Ltd 1970, 1975*

All rights reserved. No part of this publication may be reproduced, stored in a retrieval system, or transmitted in any form or by any means, electronic, mechanical, photocopying, recording, or otherwise, without the prior permission of the Copyright owner.

*First published 1970*
*Second edition 1975*

ISBN 0 582 48184 8

*Printed in Great Britain by*
*Whitstable Litho Ltd.*
*Whitstable Kent*

Aspects of modern sociology

The social structure of modern Britain

GENERAL EDITORS

John Barron Mays
Eleanor Rathbone Professor of Sociology, University of Liverpool

Maurice Craft
Senior Lecturer in Education, University of Exeter

BY THE SAME AUTHOR

Growing Up In The City (*1954*)
On the Threshold of Delinquency (*1959*)
Education and the Urban Child (*1962*)
Crime and the Social Structure (*1963*)
The Young Pretenders (*1965*)
The School in Its Social Setting (*1967*)
School of Tomorrow (*1968*) (with W. Quine and K. Pickett)
The Introspective Society (*1968*)
**Juvenile Delinquency, The Family and the Social Group (*1972*)**
The Social Treatment of Young Offenders (*1975*)

# Contents

| | |
|---|---|
| Editors' Preface | vii |
| Foreword | ix |
| 1 Introduction | 1 |
| 2 Trends and patterns | 13 |
| 3 Some theories of crime causation | 25 |
| 4 Crime and social class | 44 |
| 5 The socialization process and crime | 70 |
| 6 The aims of the penal system | 79 |
| 7 The treatment of offenders | 93 |
| 8 New trends in methods and treatment | 117 |
| 9 Conclusion | 138 |
| References and further reading | 149 |
| Criminal statistics, graphs and tables | 159 |
| Index | 169 |

# Editors' Preface

British higher education is now witnessing a very rapid expansion of teaching and research in the social sciences, and, in particular, in sociology. This new series has been designed for courses offered by universities, colleges of education, colleges of technology, and colleges of further education to meet the needs of students training for social work, teaching and a wide variety of other professions. It does not attempt a comprehensive treatment of the whole field of sociology, but concentrates on the social structure of modern Britain which forms a central feature of most university and college sociology courses in this country. Its purpose is to offer an analysis of our contemporary society through the study of basic demographic, ideological and structural features, and through the study of such major social institutions as the family, education, the economic and political structure, and so on.

The aim has been to produce a series of introductory texts which will in combination form the basis for a sustained course of study, but each volume has been designed as a single whole and can be read in its own right.

We hope that the topics covered in the series will prove attractive to a wide reading public and that, in addition to students, others who wish to know more than is readily available about the nature and structure of their own society will find them of interest.

JOHN BARRON MAYS<br>
MAURICE CRAFT

# Acknowledgements

The publishers are indebted to the following for permission to reproduce copyright materials:
J. H. Bagot and Jonathan Cape Ltd, for figure 1, taken from *Juvenile Delinquency*, 1941; *New Society* for figure 2, taken from an article by Leslie T. Wilkins, published in *New Society*, No. 42, July, 1963; The Home Office for figures 4, 5 and 6, which were taken from Home Office *Criminal Statistics*, August, 1969; Her Majesty's Stationery Office for figure 7, taken from the *Report of the Committee on the Age of Majority*, 1967; UNESCO for figure 8, taken from an article by Denis Szabó in *International Social Science Journal*, Vol. XVIII, No. 2, 1966. This figure appeared in its original form in *Sociology of Deviant Behaviour*, by Marshall Clinard, published by Holt, Rinehart and Winston.

# Foreword

This book attempts to perform a wellnigh impossible task. It seeks within the compass of some 50,000 words to deal with the nature of crime and to examine the various forms of treatment that in modern Britain have been devised to cope with and contain it.

Inevitably it has been necessary to cut corners and to deal only perfunctorily with some aspects of causation and treatment. In particular I have done scant justice to the psychological approach and have been obliged to ignore entirely the contributions of psychiatrists and psycho-analysts. I have concentrated on the more traditional sociological explanations without, however, exploring the more recent writings of authors who seek to consider crime within the much wider framework of social deviance theory. To have attempted to deal with the richness and complexity of the latter would have gone far beyond the limits imposed by the present series of introductory texts.

I would like to acknowledge the helpful criticism and suggestions that I have received in the preparation of this book from my colleague, David Lowson, who must not, however, be identified with all my opinions and evaluations. I also wish to thank Mrs Margaret Webster and Mrs Doris O'Connor for their highly efficient secretarial assistance in preparing the manuscript for press.

J. B. MAYS

# Introduction 1

*Definition of the subject*

Crimes are perhaps best thought of in the first place as breaches of the criminal law.* This is the legal approach which, it will become apparent, conflicts in several ways with the sociological approach, which is the one adopted in this book.

Offences are by tradition divided into criminal and civil. Civil offences are regarded as wrongs against individuals, termed 'torts': criminal offences are regarded as offences against the wellbeing of the community as a whole and of the monarch in particular. Criminal cases, hence, take the form of Rex or Regina *versus* Smith, while in civil cases it is Brown *versus* Jones. The distinction is not always clear, however, and in practice some overlapping occurs. A special difficulty arises from the fact that crimes are usually also committed against individual persons.

English law has for many years distinguished between two kinds of crime, namely *mala in se* and *mala prohibita*. This distinction has a religious and theological basis and is important from the criminologist's viewpoint largely because it advances the thesis that there are opposite poles, crimes, that is to say, which are always bad in themselves and those which are merely forbidden for the time being for utilitarian purposes. As I have argued elsewhere it is often possible and useful to distinguish between what may be termed 'malign' and 'benign' offences.[1]

Before a crime can be said to have been committed it must be shown that in the mind of the offender there was prior criminal intent and awareness. This is legally referred to as *mens rea*, and is a

* But only at present if committed by those over 10 years of age.

somewhat outmoded concept which the law still retains. Nowadays, however, we are obliged to add on all the available psychological knowledge about motivation and intellectual understanding before it can have very much meaning.

Crimes are divided into two legal categories, termed respectively indictable and non-indictable offences. The distinction again is juridical rather than criminological and hence is not entirely justifiable in sociological terms. A rough and ready way to distinguish between the two, however, is to think of them as 'serious' and 'trivial', although this can sometimes be very misleading.

Evaluations of the annual crime statistics are usually confined to the indictable category, but morally and socially this is highly dubious when we include in the non-indictable category such offences as cruelty to children, malicious damage, living on the earnings of a prostitute, and many motoring offences including dangerous driving, and hitherto another rapidly increasing offence—taking and driving away—an offence which can have very serious possible consequences.[2]

So far we have considered crime more or less solely as law-breaking. Before we can understand what it involves for society and for individuals, we must go beyond the solely legal definitions. Since the function of the law is to uphold a standard of behaviour which may be regarded as the ethical minimum, not the optimum, this means entering fields of speculation and embarking on moral judgements. It implies adding a sociological and even a moral component to our basic concept of what constitutes criminal behaviour itself. Lawyers and social scientists have argued for a long time about this and so far are not agreed. Even criminologists are not of a mind. Terence Morris, for example, takes me to task for adopting 'the offender rather than the offence as his point of reference'.[3] Yet I believe this is precisely what we must try to do if we are to understand the manifestations of criminal and delinquent behaviour in all their depth and fulness. A narrow legalistic definition will act as an intellectual straitjacket. We need to invoke W. I. Thomas's idea of the 'definition of the situation' into our analysis and to incorporate subjective as well as objective data in our attempt to attain a general understanding of crime and delinquency. We have to try to see (perhaps by empathy) what this illegal form of conduct means in the life and mind of the individual offender.

This brings us to a second and extended definition of crime as *an index of personal maladjustment*. It is not to be so considered in every case, of course. Nor does the fact of personal maladjustment (even where proven and of a gross character) justify or excuse or diminish the injury that the community has as a result received. An index of personal maladjustment, perhaps, is best thought of not so much as a definition of crime as of one level of understanding, one possible and additional approach to the problem (especially, of course, to the acute problem of *mala in se*).

The significance of this approach is clearly of great importance in the treatment of criminals and delinquents. It is little use imposing penalties upon people who are, for psychological reasons, impervious to punishment, or, as is occasionally the case, where individuals are hungry and eager for punishment.

A further dimension which can be added to the basic legal definition of crime, and one which greatly adds to our sophistication, might similarly be termed crime as *an index of social maladjustment*. Here it is primarily the sociological perspective that is brought into play. We mean by this that sometimes it may be meaningful to interpret the delinquencies of individuals, and more especially of groups, as arising from stresses and strains, twists and warping, generated within the structure of society itself. In this case, the focus is on the social milieu, on the social situation and its pressures and constraints on people, rather than on the individual and his psychology as such.

It can sometimes be argued, if not effectively proved, that the experience of what has come to be called 'relative deprivation' can generate criminal attitudes and promote illegal behaviour. Differentials arising from low status, unequal economic rewards, life-chances and opportunities for development and social betterment have often been indicted as fundamentally criminogenic.

It is an important aspect of the sociological approach to crime that we are often led away from the individual and his shortcomings and character defects to a consideration of society and its various institutions as the matrix within which criminal impulses are fostered and within which delinquent opportunities arise. This notion of 'the criminogenic society' is highly relevant to Sutherland's famous concept of 'white collar crime' and the ways in which some of our business and financial systems operate, which will be discussed in a later chapter.

The two extensions and further dimensions that we have added to what is the essentially legal definition of crime often—as I have hinted—bring the lawyers and more sociologically oriented criminologists into conflict. Dr Herman Mannheim in his textbook, *Comparative Criminology*, deals wisely with this in the second chapter. He concludes:

> that the term 'crime' should be used in technical language only with reference to conduct that is legally crime . . . such conduct if fully proved is crime whether it actually leads to a conviction before a criminal court . . . or not . . . . Lastly, that criminology is in no way limited in the scope of its scientific investigation to what is legally crime in a given country at a given time, and it is free to use its own classifications.[4]

*Crime and morality*

It is possible, as I have argued, to divide offences into the heinous and the more venial, or into the malignant and the more benign. The latter have a reasonable prognosis: this in fact often distinguishes juvenile delinquents from adult offenders. Juvenile offenders in fact often have a fairly good prognosis, and the great majority eventually turn into more or less law-abiding people.

The relation between crime and morality is seen to be subject to changing emphasis in public opinion. The latter is influenced by writers, thinkers, politicians, the mass media and by pressure groups such as the Howard League for Penal Reform. The Quakers have always been greatly interested in penology and the welfare of prisoners, and they have had a great influence on penal practice and reform.

Definitions of what is to be regarded as criminal, moreover, can change quite radically over the years. Crime is hence a relative concept. For example, the code of Connecticut in the seventeenth century punished 'sinful dalliance' between men and women by compulsory marriage. Moreover, during the period when the Barebones Parliament was in power, adultery was for a short time an offence punishable by death. Most courts, however, simply refused to convict on such a charge. Suicide is no longer an offence, or, rather, attempted suicide is no longer an offence. And homosexual acts when conducted in private by male adults are no longer actionable. Such acts between females never were!

The two categories, sin and crime, obviously overlap. Some behaviour forms, however, are both illegal and immoral. But there is also much uncommon ground. Crime and immorality are clearly not one and the same thing. To equate law-abidingness with morally-sound behaviour and attitude is obviously a delusion. The converse is even more obviously untrue: the mere fact of breaking a law does not make an individual immoral. Crime is fundamentally a socio-legal, and not a moral, concept. Since legal codes can be seen to change with cultures, time and place, our assessment of the seriousness of any offence (perhaps other than homicide) will inevitably be relative and flexible.

The law and a general consensus regarding morality and immorality are, however, obviously not unconnected. A law which is held in general contempt, for example, is not enforceable. Acts which are agreed on balance to be anti-social at any one time could be taken as a rough-and-ready yardstick of what are crimes. But if this idea were to be accepted, some acts which are legal now could become illegal in the future, and vice versa. Hence there exists a dynamic interplay between the legal code and what, after discussion and debate, the general moral climate of the times accepts. In an age which is said to be characterized by its 'permissiveness' we would expect to see older definitions and established codes being increasingly challenged and modified. Growing sensitivities might bring more acts into the orbit of violence, while many purely private acts of doubtful morality would be looked upon more tolerantly, especially in the field of personal and sexual relationships.

## Crime recording

Crime is recorded annually in England and Wales and, separately, in Scotland. The English and Welsh figures are made up from returns of chief constables for their own areas, and consist of crimes known to the police; and they are also derived from court records giving information about individuals charged and those found guilty. The annual Blue Book, *Criminal Statistics, England and Wales*, is our primary source of basic facts, and is used by criminologists, government officials and others for making generalizations about the state of crime and also for comparative purposes. The efficiency of the police tends to be judged by these figures, on the basis of comparisons of detection rates with former years. So, too, the condition of certain aspects of the nation's morals is often assessed by journalists and commentators on the same rudimentary comparative basis.

This would, perhaps, be reasonable if the official figures were accurate enough to be relied upon. Unfortunately, this is not the case, and it is known that there are many sources of serious error. The extent of these errors and the degree of reliability of the official figures is a vexed question of crucial importance to criminologists who might wish to make use of them to support a particular theory, as well as to public officials concerned with the efficiency of law enforcement institutions. As far as this country is concerned, we cannot go back before 1938 for any kind of comparative statistics. Up to that date it is generally agreed that the official figures were haphazardly collected and unreliable to an extent that makes their use impossible. Since 1938 efforts have been made in the direction of greater standardization in compiling the official returns. Even so, some experts maintain that they are still very inadequate and sometimes downright misleading. C. H. Rolph, for example, who was a professional police officer before becoming a criminological writer, is still so dubious about the mass of figures sent in by chief constables that he discounts the annual Blue Book as little more than 'a tabulated record of regional emotions'.[5]

In less general terms, unreliability for comparative purposes arises from three other sources—other, that is to say, than from peculiarities of the system for the collection of the figures itself. These are (a) changes in the law; (b) changes in the attitude of the public; and (c) changes in police procedures. Examples of these will be fairly obvious. Laws have changed, for instance, in recent years relating to homosexual offences and attempted suicide. But it is the increase in legislation that upsets the picture most, for example, the rapid growth in motoring offences of all sorts (which *in toto* account for more than half of all offences in any one year) which has brought us all into a state of risk.

Examples of changes in public opinion are well known, and these often relate to various sex offences. A question asked in Parliament, an interview with a bishop in the national press can lead to official concern which is transmitted like an electric current down the hierarchy to the police constable who no longer turns a blind eye to behaviour in certain public places. A classic instance showing the interaction of penal practice, public opinion and criminal statistics is the great increase in the numbers of juveniles prosecuted after the passing of the Children and Young Persons Act in 1933 (see Fig. 1).

Changes in police methods of recording have already been mentioned, and these vary regionally as well as in the same divisions over time. An imponderable individual factor operates here: bridewell sergeants have to decide in the first issue whether or not a genuine offence has been committed.

A classic case of procedures producing crime waves is afforded by Lord Trenchard's intervention while Metropolitan Commissioner in the 'thirties. Finding that local stations kept two separate books called *Crimes Reported* and *Suspected Stolen* he ordered an amalgamation, and in the following twelve-month period larceny offences in that area rose from 9,500 in 1931 to 34,780 in 1932!

Police discretion also operates. In 1966 the indictable crimes showed a drop as far as juveniles were concerned, apparently as a direct result of decisions not to prosecute, since the number of boys and girls cautioned by the police for indictable offences rose by some ten per cent over the preceding year. If the number found guilty by courts is added to those cautioned for indictable offences (presumably of a minor nature), then the total showed a slight increase over 1965.

FIGURE 1
*Persons under sixteen dealt with in juvenile courts for indictable offences. England and Wales, 1910–38*[6]

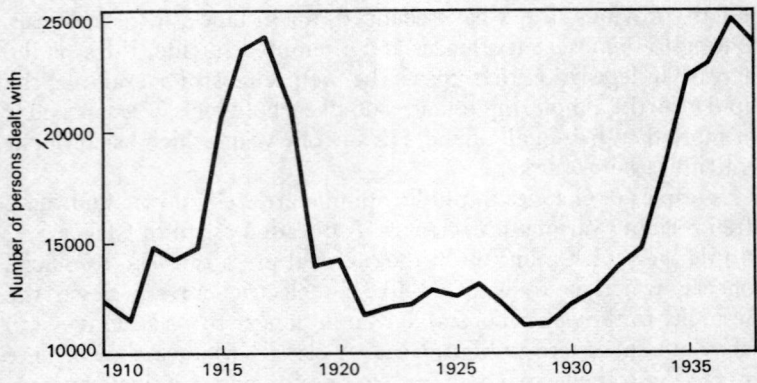

A much more important source of error is the phenomenon which we call hidden delinquency.

How great is the volume of unknown and unreported crime and delinquency? We simply don't know. We can only suppose, and it is nothing more than a supposition, that the volume of unknown crime remains fairly constant over the years. But it might not, so things may be much different from what might be supposed from construing the annual figures given in the Blue Book.

Dr Herman Mannheim has a brief but very illuminating section of his textbook devoted to a discussion of the nature and extent of the so-called 'dark' figure in the criminal statistics. He shows how certain offences, for example, indecent assaults on juveniles or homicide of the homeless, are often under-reported. There must also be an enormous volume of petty larcenies involving small sums of money or minor objects which people simply do not bother to report to the authorities. Moreover, offences committed by friends or relatives are probably often dealt with privately without recourse to the law.

Harold Silcock published a little book in 1949 which showed in a most dramatic fashion how inaccurate official statistics can be.[7] The 'black market' which characterized the immediate postwar period of extreme shortages was, he argued, nourished by substantial thefts. Silcock estimated that losses on imported and exported goods due to theft rose from £2·5 million in 1938 to the massive total of £13 million in 1948. Much of this theft was, however, unreported. Goods were merely written off as being lost in transit for, presumably, reasons of laziness, helplessness or sheer incompetence.

The amount of hidden delinquency may indeed be very great. We are all entitled to our own guesses. One estimate, which Trenaman and Emmett made some time ago now, was highly critical of conventional ways of showing the incidence of delinquency based on a given year and on a ratio between those found guilty and the population as a whole.[8] Trenaman and Emmett argued that this ratio method involved two serious weaknesses: first, it tended to mask the true extent of delinquency in the population; and, second, it exaggerated the 'accidental' element in crime. Delinquency, they claimed, may be a latent possibility with many people but never gets triggered off. Furthermore, it may occur but go undetected. Hence, 'in order to estimate the incidence of delinquency, one needs to know more than just the annual ratio of offenders to population. One needs to consider the outcropping of crime throughout the lifetime of a whole generation. One needs to know the probability of any child born at a given time becoming a delinquent some time during his life'. They went on to work out an ingenious calculation purporting to show the total lifetime delinquency of a generation between eight and eighty years of age. Their estimate was that no less than one in every nine males would become a delinquent over a whole generation, and that 'amongst those sections of the population where delinquency is found to be concentrated the proportion rises as high as one in every three' (i.e. in slums and delinquent areas). My own reading suggests that Trenaman and Emmett may not have been so very much astray, and in the notes to this chapter I have listed a number of texts and sources which, in addition to those already mentioned, seem to throw supportive light on their claim.[9]

The question now arises, since much of the available evidence depends on individuals' self-reported delinquencies, how far such memories and confessions can be trusted? One thing is certain, we will never succeed in getting behind the unreliable façade of the official statistics unless we can get people to talk freely, without restraint and without exaggeration, about their own past misdeeds. James Short Jr and Ivan Nye have discussed this in several papers.[10] They accepted the data of unreported offences which accrued through the administration of their carefully prepared questionnaire more or less at their face value, and, using it as part of their evidence, came to the conclusion that there was no significant difference between non-institutionalized boys and girls of different socio-economic strata with reference to delinquent behaviour—a view which is contrary to the common belief of most criminologists. At a later date, Dr Lee Robins, in what is likely to become an extremely influential study of sociopathic personality, used a retrospective method with her group of ex-child-guidance patients.[11] She devoted a whole chapter to the question of the validity of the material thus assembled, and concluded that 'luckily for research', "the truth, the whole truth and nothing but the truth" is seldom required to obtain useful results'. Because of her intense concern over this vital methodological problem, Robins went to the trouble of collecting as much recorded information as possible about her subjects, and this was checked up with what they said during interview. In this way she discovered not only how much under-reporting is likely, but also what form such under-reporting takes and its relation to the time elapsed between the event and the interview date. She estimated that more than two-thirds, seventy per cent, of the interviews yielded sufficient reliable information for a sociopathic diagnosis to be established. Respondents tended to minimize the extent and severity of anti-social behaviour, to push their anti-social behaviour further back in time than it actually occurred, and to suppress some of the nastier kinds of activities such as rape. Traffic offences were those most frequently admitted, which suggests that there is a pattern in self-reporting which follows fairly closely the conventional evaluation of offences. One of the most significant points which Robins makes is that complete privacy during the interview seems to have a positive effect on securing more accurate data; that if only anonymity can be guaranteed, then reliable information is much more likely to accrue, and conversely. Crimes against property, she thought, were much more easily reported than any which seemed to reflect the responddent's personal inadequacies. If this is so—and there seems to be good grounds for believing it—then we can have considerable confidence with regard to research which is concerned with the individual's past and socially less reprehensible offences. Traffic offences and thefts are, perhaps, more likely than most to be accurately and honestly recalled during interview. Other things being equal, one can safely assume that, when questioned in confidence by a *bona fide* researcher, the bulk of people will return fairly honest answers to questions even of a very personal and sensitive nature.

The available research evidence seems to suggest (*a*) that 'normal' delinquency does exist; (*b*) that much delinquency is hidden, and is unreported and unrecorded in official figures; (*c*) that a proportion of undetected delinquents are similar in their general characteristics to many actual delinquents.

Further supportive evidence may be adduced from the former operation of police juvenile liaison officer schemes in various parts of the country.[12] It is evident that many of the children dealt with by liaison officers were early and minor offenders who might otherwise have gone unknown to the authorities. Shops and chain stores were often induced to call in the help of the police juvenile liaison officer rather than drop the matter, as they might very easily have done if such a service had not been available. There is strong evidence to show that shops cannot afford to prosecute for minor thefts since this would involve members of their staff being absent for considerable periods of time while attending court, and that, in the past, provided the goods were recovered, a fair proportion of juvenile shoplifters would be sent off with a sharp warning. Furthermore, those of us engaged in education, either at school, college or university levels, know from our own experience that pupils and students who steal from one another or from the institution are very frequently dealt with internally by fines, suspensions, expulsions and other disciplinary sanctions. Moreover, those of us who can remember our own childhood can frequently recall offences of various kinds which we ourselves committed and which we were lucky enough to get away with at the time.

Indeed Dr West has commented that 'the label delinquent has become so commonplace that it can hardly signify a serious deviation from the norm in most cases.'[13]

To hazard anything more than a guess, then, regarding the extent of hidden delinquency would be extremely unwise. By its very nature, the subject must remain shrouded in mystery and obliquity. We can say, however, that some kinds of offences are more hidden than known. Professor Radzinowicz, writing in a well-known study of sex crimes, has suggested that little more than five per cent of such offences ever become publicly known.[14] If this is so, then the amount of hidden sexual delinquency must be enormous. I suspect it is. I suspect, also, that the volume of property offences of a minor and petty nature must be equally large, possibly as much again as the total of such offences known to the police. So, too, with nearly all the so-called 'white-collar' crimes. If this is true, then important moral, social and criminological questions must inevitably be raised, all of which relate to the nature of our society and which we will discuss more fully in subsequent chapters. How far, in fact, would it be true to say that crime has now emerged as a mass phenomenon and as a permanent feature of modern industrial society? And if this is so, what are the chances of a significant reduction in its incidence? And what are the lessons to be derived for those who seek to aim at its prevention rather than at its treatment?

# Trends and patterns 2

*Criminal statistics**

During the course of the past thirty years there has undoubtedly been a fairly steady increase in the amount of known crime in Great Britain. The incidence of indictable offences has more than doubled, a fact that cannot solely be accounted for in terms of population-gain over the period. Non-indictable offences have also risen, though rather less dramatically, but some (especially those non-indictable offences which, many would consider, ought to be reclassified in the indictable category such as malicious damage to property) have been increasing at an even faster rate than the allegedly more serious kinds of crime.

The volume of known offences seems, like the cost of living, almost certain to rise by a few per cent every year. In 1964, for the first time in England and Wales, it topped the million mark, and over 205,000 people were found guilty of indictable offences. The figure in the U.S.A. is between three and four time as high as in this country, with on average larger annual increases. Another, very disturbing fact is that in the U.S.A. the more serious and physically violent crimes are extremely frequent. In 1967, for instance, the F.B.I. reported over 12,000 murders in a single year, an estimated increase of 1,170 over 1966. Street rioting and racial warfare no doubt help to account for these phenomenal figures, with no less than 67 police officers killed during the course of their duties. Our overall increase in crime in the period 1966–7 was only 0·6 per cent, a matter for congratulation (strangely enough!) which has been attributed to the

---

* See pp. 159–68 for details referred to in this chapter.

appointment of more police, to rationalization of resources and amalgamation of individual forces, and to a greater degree of co-operation between police and public—the latter, perhaps, reflecting growing public concern over the volume of delinquency in contemporary society. Several propaganda campaigns were organized during this period to make the public more crime-conscious and careful with their property.

All the same, we need to bear in mind C. H. Rolph's warning that every fluctuation of the criminal statistics, either up or down, should not be treated with such exaggerated horror or relief as the case might be. 'From 0·685 to 0·7 per cent is a "crime wave". From 0·685 per cent to 0·5 per cent is a "welcome reduction in lawlessness" . . .'[1] This, of course, arises as a result of dealing with such high gross figures.

## Patterns of offences

The general overall pattern of offences over the years has, as a matter of fact, remained remarkably stable. This suggests, despite the many imperfections of the statistics, that we have some underlying constant factors which are genuinely related to social reality. Something like seventy-five per cent of all offences are larcenies, while about an additional fifth are also offences committed against property (such as breaking and fraud). In any one fairly typical year the proportion of offences against property of all kinds, hence, could be round-and-about ninety per cent. If one can venture an aside at this point, one might be tempted to say that the two great problems facing us in the criminal field today are (a) how are we going to become more honest with one another's property; and (b) how are we going to rear a new generation of safer and more law-abiding drivers?

The hard core of crimes against the person, which incidentally comprise a mere fraction of the total volume of known crime, shows some interesting changes of pattern over the years. Offences against property with violence, in which more than £100 worth of property has been stolen, have increased recently, no doubt reflecting the increasing affluence of our society as a whole. Robbery is now seen as a paying concern, as the Cambridge research study *Robbery in*

*London* has shown.[2] Howard Avison estimated that, in 1967, the proceeds of robberies within the London area alone amounted to more than £2 million.[3] Many of these offences, of course, were carried out by professional thieves and involved quite complicated planning and disposal arrangements. Higher-value thefts and robberies are increasing more rapidly at the moment than minor and petty larcenies.

Crimes of violence always arouse considerable emotional reactions and anxiety, yet they never seem to get above five per cent of the grand total. Offences of this nature categorized as 'malicious woundings' do seem to have increased, although 'felonious woundings' seem to be steady. The increase in malicious woundings may to some extent be due to changed methods of recording. That this might be so is suggested by a corresponding decrease in non-indictable assaults. While crimes of violence have doubled in the past decade or so, we must remember that all kinds of crime have shown a similar inflationary tendency. But as far as homicide goes, there has been little or no increase since, say, 1955 in the recorded incidence, in spite of the fact that the death penalty has been reduced and finally phased out during that period.

The ratio of murders per million of the population has fluctuated between 3 and 3·5 during the last decade or so, and the abolition of the death penalty in 1965 seems to have had very little influence on the incidence of homicide in Britain. There have, however, been small increases between 1966 and 1967 and again between 1967 and 1968 which could be politically exploited by those groups who seek to reinstitute the death penalty. Official Home Office figures, however, are extremely difficult to interpret and, as several writers have pointed out, temporary apparent increases are capable of being used (when suitably selected) to support both abolitionist and retentionist arguments. One of the factors which makes comparisons between different years difficult is that original charges of homicide are often subsequently reduced to manslaughter and infanticide. A great many killings, in fact, take place in the family setting; children are in greater danger from their own parents, and wives from attacks by their own husbands, than from people outside the family group.

A second regularity observable in the statistics over a long period of time is the fact that male children seem to be very much more delinquent than adults or girls. A typical offender in our society is a male juvenile of school age committing an offence with or without violence against property, or an older teenager engaged in theft, vandalism or 'hooliganism' of some variety. Current discussions of future penal policy have paid particular attention to the clear differences between adult and juvenile delinquents, a difference which often seems to be one of kind. There does indeed appear to be something particularly inept and immature about the illegal conduct of a great many young delinquents. It almost seems at times that their behaviour is largely impulsive and unthinking, more appropriate to infancy than to the demands of social realities, regressive, unsophisticated and casual. It seems as though many youngsters either drift or stumble into delinquency as a result of a disturbed, under-supervised, inadequately disciplined home and family life, but, as already indicated, their prognosis is fairly good, and by the time they reach manhood the vast majority of them have learned how to shake down to a more or less law-abiding life. A degree of delinquent behaviour as part and parcel of the growing up process (viewed both in psychological and in sociological terms) is far, then, from suggesting abnormality in childhood. Something of the order of 50 per cent and upwards of all indictable offences are committed by children and young people between the ages of ten and twenty-one—a figure which is out of all proportion to their numerical strength in the population as a whole. There is a very sharp rise in the incidence of crime and delinquency after the age of ten and up to the fourteenth birthday where the peak age for all offenders was until recently located (see Figure 7 on p. 166 below). This is followed by a falling away in later adolescence, with, however, since 1967 a secondary and now even higher peak at seventeen, and a diminution thereafter until by the age of twenty-five or so the incidence is halved. The trend is similar for boys and girls. In recent years the number of offences committed by the older adolescents, especially those round about seventeen years of age, has become very marked, reflecting perhaps to some extent a new and more truculent and anti-authority attitude on the part of a small section of the youthful population.

The fact that the peak age for offenders occurs when it does, although perhaps it might on *a priori* grounds have seemed unlikely, is nevertheless a more hopeful phenomenon than might at first appear. How much worse it would be if the peak age was found round about the age of twenty-five, if, in fact, we had a preponderance of offenders who were mentally and physically mature and so capable of producing a crop of much more serious and menacing offences than these schoolboys in their final year of formal education. The authors of the Crowther Report have, indeed, indicated that there might well be some causal connection between the fact that the peak age occurred at fourteen since, a few years earlier, when the school-leaving age was one year below that, the peak age occurred at thirteen.[4] In 1974 the school-leaving age was raised for all pupils to sixteen and it would have been extremely interesting to see if the peak age had thereafter risen by an additional year. However, changes in methods of recording and, more importantly, changes in ways of dealing with juveniles have temporarily, at least, disturbed the statistics so that it is no longer possible to note firm trends. It will, in fact, be some considerable time before we can once again derive much meaning from official crime figures. Nevertheless, we probably have enough evidence to suggest that there is something psychologically disturbing about the final year of formal education which could in certain cases result in delinquent behaviour. It is reasonable to suppose that a minor crisis of identity with subsequent loss of nerve may occur at this stage of a child's biography, and that difficult or even delinquent behaviour at this period often serves as a kind of safety valve for the release of tension and anxiety. And it might, perhaps, not be too fanciful to suggest that the second peak now showing at seventeen represents a similar later crisis of nerve and identity, brought about this time, not by a realization that the world of childhood is rapidly coming to an end, but by a realization that the sands of youth itself are not unlimited and that, in a very few years' time, the boy will be faced with the onset of full legal majority and the near certainty of marriage and family responsibilities.

These are, of course, at the moment little more than speculations, but clearly they point to areas of stress and special difficulty to which our research interests ought to be turning with increasing attention.

The third and final generalization we can make from a study of the criminal statistics over a period of time is again an obvious and well-known one. It is simply that men are much more criminal in their behaviour than women, and boys much more delinquent than girls. Young girls are even more law-abiding than their own mothers, so it seems.

At younger ages girls are about ten times less delinquent than boys, although in adolescence the gap is narrowed a little to about six to one. Girls also fall away from their peak at fourteen much more rapidly than boys, suggesting an earlier age of maturity. This phenomenon has never been completely explained and accounted for. Barbara Wootton has drawn our attention to it on several occasions in the past twenty years. She says rather sweetly, speaking about adult offenders: '... while for many years overcrowding in men's prisons has been a persistent nightmare, a not infrequent problem in Holloway Gaol has been the lack of sufficient inmates to keep the place clean'.[5]

Some tentative suggestions have been put forward to account for this remarkable difference between males and females in relation to their attitudes to law-keeping. The most plausible in my view is related to differential social roles which our society prescribes for men and women. To attribute the differences solely to physiological make-up and biological functions would be to ignore the significance of social norms and social prescriptions in accounting for human behaviour. Men are expected to be pugnacious; even in childhood they are encouraged, sometimes even compelled, to take part in highly aggressive forms of sport. They are also expected to be highly competitive (a disguised form of aggression). This prepares them for their future roles as the family breadwinners and defenders of the nation. Girls are expected to indulge in quieter games involving dolls and prams, and from a very early age they seem to identify with their mothers. Effeminate boys and mannish girls are derided because they patently upset the conventional stereotypes. The male pacifist is an intolerable freak and in some societies he is treated as an enemy of the community and punished harshly.

The American criminologist, Gresham Sykes, in an interesting general essay on crime, sums up the social role argument and interpretation in this way:

> Before you leap to the conclusion that man's physical nature is a source of criminality, let us note two things: (1) although most criminals are probably male, most males are probably not criminals; and (2) differences in the behaviour of men and women in our society far transcend the biological differences between the sexes.[6]

He goes on to argue that, if this social interpretation is true, then, as the social status of men and women becomes more nearly alike, their crime rates should become similar. And, indeed, a number of comparisons bear out this line of reasoning. During the years of the Second World War, according to Sykes, women in the United States came to hold a social position more nearly like that of men, and the difference between their crime rates decreased accordingly.

Sutherland has maintained a similar point of view:

> The significant difference is in the social positions of the girls and women as compared with the boys and men, and the difference in social positions either determines the frequency and intensity of the delinquency and anti-delinquency patterns which impinge upon them or determines the frequency of opportunities for crimes which are available to them.[7]

More recently, it seems, girls have been trying to catch up with their brothers. Although boys are still very much more delinquent, the crime rate for girls has about doubled. Girls have also been found guilty of violence against the person and even of 'muggings', which seems to imply that sexual equality is tending to make the offences of females more akin to those of males than was the case in former years.

## Opportunity and crime

The fact that crime is a growth industry in modern affluent societies should not surprise us, for there is an obvious connection between theft and opportunity. One category of offence which does seem sociologically specific enough to use diagnostically in this connection is, as Leslie Wilkins has pointed out, larceny from shops (where presumably much more merchandise is available for pilfering than hitherto). Similarly, the offence of larceny from vehicles could be used in combination to illustrate a similar sociological trend, while, as an index of generally increasing affluence, the number of private motor vehicles registered could be employed. Wilkins has in fact done this in the graph reproduced in Fig. 2.[8]

**FIGURE 2**
*Trends in theft*

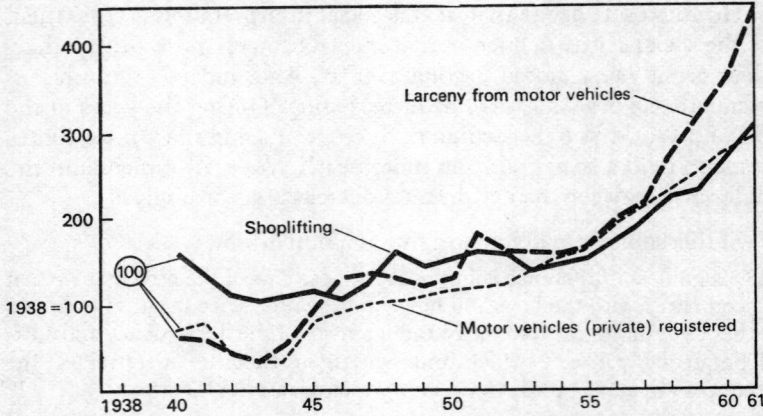

As he shows, the three trends are remarkably similar, although thefts from motors is more closely related to the numbers of vehicles on the roads. Wilkins adds:

If one feels any lack of surprise that these trends are highly correlated and sees nothing remarkable in the fact that thefts from motor vehicles follow closely the number of vehicles, it would be interesting to inquire why this result was expected, and how this expectation squares up with one's philosophy of criminal behaviour and the action which it is believed should be taken to protect society. Following the strict moralistic view, it is difficult to explain why more cars should mean more stealing from cars, *unless it is postulated that our moral standards deteriorate proportionally to the number of motor vehicles.* There is no evidence that any other form of criminal behaviour has been displaced by the increase in thefts from vehicles.

Crime in our comparatively affluent and increasingly permissive society (to use two popular epithets which, though perhaps difficult to define, are almost certainly meaningful to most of us) is clearly closely related to the opportunity structure and the growth of temptation. Now if this is so, and the evidence seems on the whole to indicate that it is the case, then we are obliged to concede that much crime has a rational basis and is explicable in terms of normal psychology. In other words, there is an element of calculation involved in the bulk of offences which, of course, are committed against property and consist in a variety of attempts to convert other people's goods and money for our own unlegitimated use.

This naturally brings up the question of organized professional crime on the American gangster and Mafia model. And is professional crime on the increase? Certainly the execution of well thought out and highly profitable crimes in the way of raids on jewellers, pay-bag snatches and similar robberies, and growing opportunities in connection with the extortion of protection money since the legalization of gambling and the setting up of gaming clubs in this country, suggest that new opportunities could be attracting more persistent and career-minded villains. The gang which planned and executed the famous mail-train robbery in Buckinghamshire in 1963 and got away with over £2 million (most of which, incidentally has never been recovered) typify this hitherto rare kind of organized crime most alarmingly. Nearly all of these men are now in prison serving dauntingly long sentences, but even there, as events have shown, they are still capable of organizing and executing ingenious and successful escapes with the help of friends outside and, presumably, not identified. Howard Avison estimates that so far in this country 'there are probably no more than two or three hundred criminal leaders and professional receivers'. Together he reckons that they would not be responsible for more than 8,000 principal crimes each year. 'However, one of the outstanding characteristics of the way in which organized criminals work is the large number of subsidiary crimes they commit, such as the theft of explosives, cutting equipment, cars and vans, and possibly even money for the payment of gang members to be recruited in the future.' This implies that a great many minor and petty offenders are involved in fringe activities connected with the execution of these big-scale robberies. Such men could be inadequate personalities, in the psychological sense; men with damaged egos resulting from emotional deprivations in childhood or even in later life, members of that grey fraternity of habitual criminals and recidivists who spend half their lives in and out of various penal institutions and who are such an abiding nuisance to the police and prison officials since they seem to be more or less immune to treatment and incapable of social rehabilitation. They are the jackals of the trade, the hangers-on and near-group members who are paid to participate as and when they are useful but, in the main, are regarded as expendables, living only on the dropped crumbs of crime.

Avison has further estimated that something in the region of £50 million is stolen annually, often in large and well-planned coups. If we remember that the detection rate for indictable offences, over the whole range, is seldom more than 40 per cent, then we can see why 'With profits so high and risks so low, it is inevitable that a new class of professional criminal should emerge'.

The question of how far this professional adult crime system operates in Britain and what its relationship is, if any, with juvenile delinquents and what the journalists are apt, all too loosely, to call gangs, is an interesting and important issue that will be discussed later when we come to look at subcultural theories and, in particular, when we come to consider the theories of Cloward and Ohlin.

Two further trends may be briefly referred to here, both of which seem to relate more to young people than to children or to adults, and which give some statistical support to the notion that is sometimes expressed that our present teenage generation is unusually unruly and delinquency-prone. These are drunkenness and drug-taking. Drunkenness does seem to be on the increase, surely a further result of more people having more money in their pockets to spend on personal indulgences and luxuries. Since the mid-nineteen-fifties the number of prosecutions for drunkenness has gone up by 40 per cent (see Table on p. 168 below). Not only have more men been found guilty of this offence but there has been a noticeable increase in the numbers of young people being prosecuted. As the figures show very clearly, drunkenness is becoming increasingly common amongst teenagers and even amongst those who are not legally entitled to drink in public.

Drug-taking, which is illegal for those not under the care and treatment of a physician, has not been accurately reported for very long, but some idea of the increase in recent years may be judged by the fact that convictions for offences controlled by the Dangerous Drug Act in respect of cannabis went up from 663 in 1963 to 3,071 in 1968, and that convictions in respect of manufactured drugs such as heroin went up in the same period from 63 to 1,099. Furthermore, in 1960 there was only one addict under twenty years of age known to the Home Office, whereas by 1968 there were 764. The Brain Committee and various other reports which in recent years have looked into the subject of drug-addiction, seem to agree that young people are more prone to this habit than in earlier years and that greater financial means, coupled with an increase in the number of illegal sources of supply for marijuana and the amphetamines at a time of growing public tolerance or apathy, have contributed to the emergence of this new but far-from-widespread problem. Estimates of the total numbers of people who could fairly be designated as narcotic addicts have been made between 2,000 and 3,000, most of whom are believed to live in the London conurbation.[9] It is not uncommon for pop stars to be found indulging illegally in such drugs as marijuana, or pot, and there is clearly a danger that unstable youngsters will follow their example in order to indulge in psychedelic experiments. It is by no means certain, however, whether or not recourse to hallucinogenic drugs does any long-term harm. Nor are we at all sure that transition from the so-called soft drugs to the hard drugs like heroin is the likely outcome of the addictive process.

There are indeed indications that 'pot culture' may now in the mid-nineteen-seventies be on the wane, and that alcohol may be taking its place as a group activity for the older adolescents. This seems to suggest that the campaign to legalise cannabis was misguided or at least unnecessary. The Misuse of Drugs Act 1971, which came into force in 1973, made a distinction between supplying drugs and having them in one's possession, the former attracting the more severe prison sentence, with anything up to fourteen years for drug trafficking or smuggling. Mere possession, on the other hand, is much more leniently treated, indicative of the tolerance of a generally more 'permissive' society.

# Some theories of crime causation 3

Early attempts to unravel and describe the causes of crime in terms of one main explanatory theory in the end resulted in failure. One of the most influential in its day was the Lombrosian, sometimes known also as the Italian, school, which maintained that criminals were determined by their heredity and could be distinguished from non-criminals by certain clear physical stigmata.

Another widely supported interpretation was that which stressed the importance of imitation in criminal causation. This school, associated with the name of the French psychologist, Gabriel de Tarde, existed at the end of the nineteenth century more or less as an alternative explanation to that of the Lombrosians. Neither viewpoint is entirely discredited or extinct today, and modern versions, stressing either criminally-disposed somatypes or the imitative aspects of delinquent behaviour, are still discernible in the writings of, for example, Sheldon and Eleanor Glueck, W. H. Sheldon and Edwin Sutherland. They are not so much wrong as over-simplified interpretations of varieties of human behaviour which are obviously heterogeneous and of an extremely complex nature. Modern theories of multiple causation which make use of insights and concepts derived from a wide variety of social sciences are more acceptable to contemporary criminologists who would claim that there is no one universal cause of crime but many different causes or related causal factors. There are, in fact, a number of criminal types and a variety of types of crime—all of which need to be sorted out and documented by future research workers. But the search for the single general causal principle is doomed to failure—'One might as well', wrote Barbara Wootton, 'look for some equally simple "cause" to account for the presence in Piccadilly of all the people who happen to be there at any particular moment.'[1]

25

There are, however, a number of general sociological and socio-cultural theories about the nature of crime and its meaning in modern societies which can be used as a backcloth against which more detailed and specific explanations can be studied and evaluated.

Sociologists not unexpectedly stress the social element in criminal conduct and this has led them at times into heated and unprofitable verbal warfare with other social scientists, particularly with psychologists and psychoanalysts. Sutherland, for example, in his well-known study of *White Collar Crime*, wrote of the 'current tendency ... to advocate emotional instability as the trait which explains ordinary criminal behaviour', and went on jocularly to ask whether we are to think that 'the crimes of the Ford Motor Company are due to the Oedipus Complex, or those of the Aluminium Company of America to an Inferiority Complex, or those of the U.S. Steel Corporation to Frustration and Aggression, or those of Du Pont to Traumatic Experience, or those of Montgomery Ward to Regression to Infancy?'[2]

But we must try to maintain a position of balance between two opposite points of view which would assert that (a) individual psychological traits are always the most *fundamental* causes of crime; and (b) delinquency is a *purely* socio-legal concept. The sociologist stresses the fact that without the existence of a social system crime as we know it could not exist. Criminal behaviour can, of course, for analytical purposes sometimes be considered apart from the social context in which it occurs, but, if we are thinking about crime in general, then we are obliged to consider the social structure of which it forms an indispensable part. And law and the legal framework and the process of prosecution and the imposition of sanctions are also part of the structure of society and exist to control the standards of common behaviour and to set certain minimal norms for social conduct.

Human beings, unlike some of the lower creatures such as ants, are obliged to learn the agreed conduct pattern from scratch. The rules have to be internalized; the norms have to be assimilated and made our own. As Jackson Toby wrote, 'The fact that the rules have to be *learned* makes crime possible; the fact that situations of extraordinary temptation arise makes crime inevitable.'[3]

Here we again see how the sociologist lays stress on the concept of 'opportunity'. Opportunity and temptation are closely associated. So, too, for the sociologist, as of course for a great many psychologists also, <u>crime is essentially learned behaviour</u>. Learned, that is to say, by association with other delinquents and acquired by imitation of the observed and sometimes admired delinquent behaviour. By the same token, if anything interferes with the learning process associated with socially acceptable behaviour, this, too, could be thought of as sometimes resulting in delinquency. Forms of conduct appropriate to infancy and childhood can, if prolonged into later developmental stages, sometimes bring a young person or even an adult into conflict with the law.

*Crime and immaturity*

Dr Roper has succinctly expressed the connection between delinquency and immaturity in this way:

The question presents itself: if criminality and immaturity are so closely associated, may they not be much the same thing? We know that young children can be seen, in any not too tidy nursery, assaulting each other, taking the belongings of others, and even engaging in sexual exploration, in a way which would be criminal in adults. No sensible person worries about these things because he knows that it is a normal phase of development which will disappear with training. May it not be that criminality is merely the persistence or reappearance of this nursery stage of development, which becomes ugly and dangerous simply because of the greater strength and sophistication of the adult? After all, it is natural enough to want to have what one desires as quickly and simply as possible, and it takes training to regard a more devious proceeding as proper. We know, too, that some kinds of minor criminality are frequent enough amongst quite ordinary people. May it not be, therefore, that criminality is the 'natural' condition of man and that we are all latent criminals, proof against ordinary temptations only because we have been taught to wait for what we want and to abhor the direct methods of the criminal?[4]

Here again we see how sociological and psychological theories and explanations complement and overlap one another. The actual process of learning may perhaps be more narrowly the province of the psychologist but the content of learning is the especial focus of interest for the sociologist.

## Delinquent contacts

Moreover, other people's attitudes can also be conducive to law-breaking and delinquency. If those we come into daily contact with are criminalistic in their outlook (even though their own conduct may remain narrowly within legal bounds), they can exert a criminogenic influence upon us by the fact that we know that they challenge the validity of the legal code and from the fact that we know that they will be sympathetic toward us if we are found out in delinquent acts.

Different social groups and people living in different social milieux will have different norms and standards. Some will be more tolerant than others of breaches of the law; some will accept small and petty stealing as everyday occurrences; others will take a highly moralistic and condemnatory attitude towards petty theft but be blandly tolerant of 'sharp' practices in business by which they or others acquire a great deal of profit.

It all depends on how individuals and the groups with which they are associated define the situation, i.e. do they see a form of conduct as natural, and so acceptable, at their level, or do they see it as an outrage to their moral standards? This matter of the differential definition of a situation is one of crucial importance in criminology because whether or not individuals define or think of themselves as criminals or just as people down on their luck offers an important clue to their possible social rehabilitation if they have been in prison or borstal, for instance. Once a man has defined his own role as that of 'enemy of society' or of a social outcast, then it will be accordingly much harder to bring him back into the everyday life of the community without further delinquent breakdown.

## The normality of crime

Sociologists think of crime not only as learned but also as comparatively normal behaviour. Normal here has several meanings.

One is that it can be thought of as being normal for a member of a specific group which defines acceptable and unacceptable behaviour in certain ways which are in conflict with the general social and legal codes of the wider society. This interpretation is one which the subcultural theorists have exploited in recent years with considerable success, especially in their understanding of the nature of juvenile delinquency and in their analyses of the adolescent gang.

But there is also a body of sociological writing which has postulated the 'scandalous' idea that crime is normal in a more general sense than suggested above. It is not merely that certain groups are delinquency-prone and delinquency-tolerant or downright criminalistic in their outlook, but that *crime itself is a normal social phenomenon.* Durkheim first expounded this revolutionary view which was based on his conviction that crime performed a useful and a necessary social function. In his well known book, *The Rules of the Sociological Method*, he wrote: 'To classify crime amongst the phenomena of normal sociology is not to say merely that it is an inevitable, though regrettable phenomenon, due to the incorrigible wickedness of men: it is to affirm that it is a factor in public health, an integral part of all healthy societies'.[5]

This view may be compared with Dr Alex Comfort's statement:

When, therefore, scientific psychiatry is deliberately invoked, as it is today, to deal with individual crime, it must inevitably become widely involved in the study of non-criminal forms of delinquency upon which patterns of centralized society have come to depend, since both the demand and the supply of delinquents may be held to be products of that society. The convicted criminal represents, to this extent, not so much an eliminable by-product of our culture as a divergent surplus of one of its manufactures.[6]

Durkheim went on to argue first that the conditions of which crime is an integral part are indispensible to the normal evolution of law and social morality, allowing the individual to express himself and thereby to make an original contribution to the community. This freedom to express one's own unique view of the world admits both Socrates and Al Capone and perhaps we cannot have one without the other. His second point, which he developed in *The*

*Division of Labour in Society*, is that public sentiments are reinforced when crimes occur and that the principal function of punishment is not—as might commonly be supposed—the reformation of the offender and the infliction of a just penalty on the individual criminal, but the reinforcement of our collective values.[7] By taking action together against criminals we become more conscious of our social bonds and more united as a community.

Durkheim's views have more sociological than penological value. They do indeed help us to understand some of the profundities which lie below the surface of social life and to appreciate the enormous number of cross-currents, latent functions and countervailing influences which a typical common-sense view of social behaviour is almost certain to ignore and deny. They may be compared with the position of the well-known American writer and criminologist, Sheldon Glueck, a man who has devoted his whole life to the study of crime, who seriously argues that it is not criminal behaviour but non-criminal behaviour that requires explanation.[8] Crime, in Glueck's view, is the natural, as it were unredeemed, condition of man. Several psycho-analysts seem to hold more or less the same view. Edward Glover, for example, claims that '... *crime is part of the price paid for the domestication of a naturally wild animal*, or, to put it more cautiously, that crime is *one* of the results of unsuccessful domestication'.[9] Other consequences, of course, would be the neuroses.

If such a view is correct, it would seem to imply that civilization is only skin-deep, that it is the law and its associated forms of social constraint which prevent and inhibit the aggressive and egotistical impulses of individuals from having free rein. At the moment no proofs can be adduced to settle this issue one way or another. My own view is that it is wrong, or should I say that I am emotionally reluctant to admit that the natural habitat of man is the jungle? I would say that the impulse of love and the desire for consensus is of equal, if not, in the final analysis, greater moment than either rampant individualism or naked lust for power or for sexual licence. I would have thought, too, that even sociological Marxists, who seem to favour revolutionary action and who stress the importance of conflict in social relations, were, by their broader ideology, committed to some final happy state of society in which the poisons of individualism (fostered and sustained by the evil capitalist system) are finally neutralized in the benign state of social nirvana in which identification with and immersion in the total life of the whole community is ultimately consummated.

Be that as it may, we were saying with reference to Durkheim that his view that crime is to be regarded as normal in modern societies grew partly from the statistically obvious fact of its widespread nature and its generality, and also from the more subtle fact that it performs certain very useful social functions. Durkheim's second major contribution to criminological theory stemmed from his concept of *anomie* which he worked out in very great detail in connection with his comparative study of suicide in differently constituted societies.

Very briefly, his research seemed to indicate that in societies where social standards and restraints were slackening a condition of *normlessness* occurred which could account for a rise in suicide rates and a higher incidence of this offence in less stable and less integrated communities.[10] More specifically, the insatiable hunger in capitalist economies for more goods, money and property—stimulated by modern mass advertising and salesmanship—fosters this endemic discontent for more and more personal possessions. In fact, certain American criminologists have indicted this whole social system itself as being basically criminogenic. Moreover, it is not without significance that the United States, which is the richest and the most individualistic of modern capitalist societies, has also produced an underworld of nation-wide, highly-organized professional crime without parallel in any other country. American authors have inveighed against the criminal network of professional racketeers, the system of graft and political corruption which is intimately keyed in with big business and even the administration of justice. Everyday affairs and attitudes have come in for censure. For example, Donald Taft said in his textbook, *Criminology*:

American culture is, even if decreasingly, the embodiment of materialism. The dollar is dominant if not almighty. The symbol of success is still what

Veblen called conspicuous consumption. Honest dollars may be preferred to dishonest dollars, but not a few unearned dollars *have* brought prestige.[11]

The discussion of 'white-collar crime' which follows in this chapter and the various instances of public scandals in this country which will be cited seem to point the same way. High crime rates do seem to be causally related to a nation's economic growth and productivity.

The ultimate logic of the kind of analysis and critical examination made of modern societies by such writers as Taft, William Foote Whyte,[12] Marshall Clinard[13] and many others reinforces the essentially Durkheimean view that crime in a great many instances should be thought of as behaviour which is normal in both the sociological and psychological senses of the word. Not only are some aspects of the ordinary everyday social processes strongly criminogenic but the organization of crime on a businesslike footing has resulted in the creation of criminal networks into whose orbit many otherwise 'respectable' citizens and vulnerable children and youths are inevitably drawn. Crime, then, to quote my own words, 'is, if not inevitable, always a potentiality in social life which very frequently becomes an actuality'.[14]

*White-collar crime*

This important concept was invented by the late Edwin H. Sutherland and quickly became an integral part of criminological theory. Briefly, he described white-collar crimes as 'crimes committed by persons of respectability and high social status in the course of their occupations'.[15] We must emphasize the 'persons of respectability and high social status' in this connection, because this delimits the use of the concept to what we may think of as more or less middle-class offenders. These are pre-eminently business crimes, contraventions of trade regulations, embezzlement, fraudulent conversion of money or property etc., and they are usually committed by such people as solicitors, financiers, managers and executives, accountants and higher grade clerks and officials. Of course such middle-class white-collar offenders can also commit the run-of-the-mill offences against property and against the person, but very often their only known offences are the ones carried out in connection with their business or professional activities. Lower-class people quite obviously are not so frequently exposed to the same kinds of temptation. It was a matter about which Sutherland became indignant, since he showed how in a great many instances both individuals and corporations committed their white-collar crimes without being detected, or even if detected, without having to endure the stigma of a criminal prosecution.

Sutherland's researches in this field extended the frontiers of conventional criminology and have led to much discussion and speculation by theorists, although, so far, it does not seem to have been possible to bring white-collar crime easily within the ambit of one explanatory theory about the nature of crime in general.

Cressey defends Sutherland against the attack that he was trying to extend the concept of crime into muzzy additional dimensions and thereby change and confuse the whole nature of the concept.[16] He was, Cressey argues, treating white-collar crimes as crimes, i.e. as violations of the criminal law,* but with this crucial difference; that, for what must be purely social and class reasons, in a great many cases, having defined white-collar offences as crimes, legislatures provide methods for dealing with them which are very different from procedures prescribed for other kinds of crime. In other words, the offenders are dealt with by special procedures which suggest that they are not really criminals at all. Sutherland cites the Sherman Antitrust Law and other similar laws as an example of this curious tenderness towards middle-class offenders and offences. As a more recent commentator puts it, 'White-collar crime has the veneer of respectability born of community tolerance.'[17] It is 'conventional delinquent behaviour' for a certain social class and group, just like a limited amount of 'knocking-off' is in other social classes and occupational groups.

Sutherland's main evidence is culled from an examination of the criminal records of seventy large American corporations during their

*Although it is admitted that Sutherland was not always consistent in this respect and did occasionally seem to go beyond his original basic definition.

life careers which were, on average, approximately forty-five years. Such crimes were persistent and more extensive than prosecutions indicate; moreover, the individuals who were prosecuted suffered no loss of status among their business associates (a violation of the criminal code is not *ipso facto* a violation of the business code). Furthermore, such business men often openly expressed contempt for the law and for government itself. 'The business man's contempt for law, like that of the professional thief, grows out of the fact that the law impedes his behaviour.'

White-collar crimes are not only deliberate, they are organized. Yet these offenders do not conceive of themselves as criminals. Even when they are brought to justice they are always defended as men of high reputation, honour and respectability:

The white-collar criminal does not conceive of himself as a criminal because he is not dealt with under the same official procedures as other criminals and because, owing to his class status, he does not engage in intimate personal association with those who define themselves as criminals.

*Examples of white-collar crime*

Many offences of this kind never get recorded: tax-evasion is often dealt with administratively by revenue officials and embezzlements from firms and companies may be dealt with privately. Moreover, the fact that most white-collar crimes are committed against public bodies or large amorphous groups such as the tax-payers tends to increase public tolerance of them. So the official criminal statistics fail to reveal the vast area of white-collar crime. Our view of crime persistently remains unidimensional and class biased: 'We will continue to visit heavy penal sanctions on the persistent petty thief while the persistent petty embezzler will tend to avoid the clutches of the criminal law.'[18]

But white-collar offences can sometimes also be thought of as an extension to Sutherland's theory in terms of the kind of offences committed rather than of the kind of person committing them. A good example of this is the tax evasion at the present time committed by immigrants from India and Pakistan (who are almost by definition of comparatively low social status) defrauding the inland revenue by claiming allowances for non-existent dependent relatives in their country of origin. This is estimated at present to be costing us between £5 and £7 million a year and has been debated in Parliament following the publication of the all-party panel of M.P.s who sit on the Public Accounts Committee.

A not atypical example of corrupt business practice is afforded by a recent case in which it became known that an oil company representative was asking for £500 from a firm wishing to obtain permission to erect a new petrol filling station. He stated that he required this sum of money in order to bribe members of the city council committee to accept the application and so secure the concession.

Marshall B. Clinard's book, *The Black Market*, massively documents the extent and depth of the black market in America during two major modern wars. The black market operated at all three levels of production, distribution and retailing of goods. It was not confined to scarce or rationed commodities, although wartime exigencies produced a big black market in gasolene and meat. Control of scarce commodities made counterfeiting of coupons profitable and rife. Landlords meanwhile, cashing in on scarcity of property demanded hidden rents in the form of key money and other trickeries. Said Clinard, '... a survey of violations has indicated that the black market was not the outgrowth of unique conditions of any particular industry, the peculiar injustice of certain regulations, the squeeze at a particular level of trade, or the conditions prevailing in certain parts of the country', but basically '... appears to have been related to many practices current among certain elements in business during peacetime'. Many businessmen, for instance, argued that the government had no right whatsoever to interfere with trade and commerce and that there should be no bar of any kind placed upon individual enterprise: 'There was a fairly prevalent belief that desires for profits generally should not be curbed, even in a national emergency.' Clinard alleged that blackmarketeering extended throughout every class of society and at all levels of the national life, ranging from traditional sharp practices to attempts at large-scale conspiracy.

Our argument is now converging on definitions of morality and immorality, which, at the psychological level, are closely connected with how individuals perceive themselves. White-collar criminals seem to exhibit attitudes towards their offences which are almost certainly culturally-induced with regard to what is and what is not really crime. G. E. Levens, in an article entitled '101 White-collar Criminals', said:

One cannot escape the impression that most of the star prisoners in the sample did not conceive of themselves as criminals. This epithet still conveyed to them, as to most people, the image of the thug, the bank robber, the demoniacal and notorious villain who clubs old ladies in dark alleys and makes off with the housekeeping: the sort of person, in fact, with whom they were now obliged to live every day but from whom they continued to distinguish themselves, even while sharing the same cell.[19]

In addition to white-collar crime it is also worth considering the impact of what we may call, for want of a better term, 'wickedness in high places' and those public scandals which are headlined and widely discussed in all the media. The knowledge that well-known and highly-respected members of society are also guilty of offences against the law and against the moral code must surely have some weakening effect upon general standards of behaviour and give some encouragement to those who have broken the law to justify themselves with the reassuring idea that 'everyone's on the fiddle' and 'society itself is bent'.

The notorious case of Dr Ward and the widely reported Profumo affair of a few years ago, accounts of the two-way mirror in Ward's flat enabling voyeurism to take place with impunity, and the riotous parties at Cliveden, lifted the veil from a most sordid round of upper-class sexual orgies and criminal intrigues.

Then, on an entirely different level, there was the Ballot Box Trickery in 1961 when the election to the secretaryship of the E.T.U. was effected by ballot rigging. A High Court enquiry, after sitting in judgement, ordered a re-election and another candidate was, this time legitimately, returned.

The world of finance and big business affords some notorious examples of accepted behaviour which sometimes, although within the law, clearly offends against the canons of decency and honest dealing. Certain exaggerated forms of advertising; the takeover bids whereby one big firm or combine extends its empire and interests by offering financial inducements to shareholders, and sometimes golden handshakes to departing directors of the assimilated firms, regardless of the jobs and interests of employees; stock exchange speculation whereby it apparently is possible to buy shares or goods you have no intention of paying for, and of selling goods or shares that you do not even possess; bond-washing (a form of tax evasion which consisted of selling government stock a few weeks before the dividend is due *cum-dividend* and buying them back later much more cheaply *ex-dividend*) only recently stamped out by legislation—these, and similar pocket-lining practices by financiers and businessmen, must make the ordinary citizen feel frustrated, to say the least, and almost despairing about ever seeing obviously anti-social behaviour brought under legal control and finally outlawed. Moreover, as a tax-payer, he must have read in astonishment of the excessive profits made by the Ferranti Company in contracts with the Ministry of Aviation for making the Bloodhound I missile. Eventually parliamentary questions led to an enquiry and the voluntary return to the exchequer of several million pounds by the company. But the irksome query remains: how often are government contracts in fact handled in this grossly hit and miss way by civil servants and industrialists?

Were space available it would be possible to cite example after example of dubious business practices of this nature and of instances of public figures being found out in the commission of crimes and immoral acts. Clearly there is enough evidence now available for it to be no longer tenable to claim that there are two distinct types of people—the criminals and the non-criminals. Crime seems to be coterminous with society. It is, as has been well said, society's own sickness, and we are all throughout our lives either actual or potential delinquents. Such a perspective, although not yet generally accepted, has important consequences for the treatment and disposal of law-breakers, and has undoubtedly given considerable impetus to recent drives for penal reform.

## Differential association

Edwin Sutherland who, on any view, must be regarded as one of the world's major criminological thinkers, was akin to Durkheim in so far as he, too, seemed to believe that crime is inherent in all modern societies and is an essential element in the overall socio-cultural process. Delinquency is closely related to other forms of non-conformist behaviour and is likely to arise in any conflict situation produced by social disorganization. Over the years he developed and enunciated a number of propositions which have in combination come to be called the theory of differential association. The first formalization of this theory was made in the third edition of his classic textbook, *Principles of Criminology*. Although Sutherland is said not to have realized it at the outset, his differential association theory is the first or one of the earliest general explanations of the nature of crime which can claim to be mainly derived from sociological data and analysis.

Sutherland's theory may be baldly stated in terms of the following seven propositions:

1. The processes which result in systematic criminal-behaviour are fundamentally the same in form as the processes which result in systematic lawful behaviour.
2. Systematic criminal behaviour is determined in a process of association with those who commit crimes, just as systematic lawful behaviour is determined in a process of association with those who are law-abiding.
3. Differential association is the specific causal process in the development of systematic criminal behaviour.
4. The chance that a person will participate in systematic criminal behaviour is determined roughly by the frequency and consistency of his contacts with the patterns of criminal behaviour.
5. Individual differences among people in respect to personal characteristics or social situations cause crime only as they affect differential association or frequency and consistency of contacts with criminal patterns.

6. Cultural conflict is the underlying cause of differential association and therefore of systematic criminal behaviour.
7. Social disorganization is the basic cause of systematic criminal behaviour.

'Cultural conflict', says Donald Cressey in his essay on Sutherland's writings, 'is a specific aspect of social disorganization and in that sense the two concepts are names for smaller and larger aspects of the same thing.'[20]

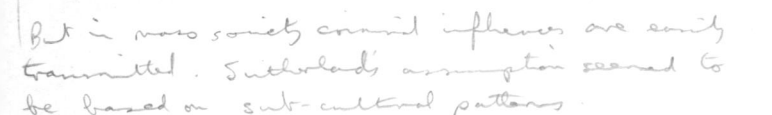

Very succinctly, Sutherland's theory seems to add up to the statement that, if an individual is exposed to more criminal than non-criminal influences in his immediate environment, his chances of breaking the law are greatly increased, and vice versa. Perhaps an ardent disciple of Sutherland might argue that it is quite impossible to conceive of any individual breaking the law who has not come into contact with criminal influences, and, conversely, that an individual who has been totally encompassed by law-abiding influences would never break the law. In so far as the essence of Sutherland's differential association theory seems to be that crime is the cause of crime many critics find it merely tautologous, academically question-begging and simply redundant. Cressey has defended Sutherland vigorously in the essay from which quotation has already been made, asserting that the currently popular 'multiple factor' theory of criminal causation is nothing but 'a philosophy of scientific despair'. However, even he doubts whether in such cases as violations of financial trusts, for instance, the differential association can ever hope to be validated empirically since the scientist would need to be able to know about every contact that the violator had made over almost his entire lifetime. Nevertheless taking what are the 'hard' facts about crime in America which a general explanatory theory must fit—i.e. that the crime rate for youth is higher than for groups in later life; that the crime rate is higher for men than for women; higher also for Negroes than for whites; higher for the native-born than for the foreign-born; higher in urban than in rural areas and for working class than for higher social groups—he thinks he can show that none of the other theories, such as personality characteristics of offenders or poverty, for example, 'fit *all* the ratios and variations as well as does the theory of differential association and differential social organization'.

In spite of many criticisms and obvious imperfections in Sutherland's propositions, it is a valuable contribition to criminology because it keys in with many other research findings and can be utilized in the preparation of practical policies for treatment and, more particularly, of prevention. As Leslie Wilkins has pointed out, following Glaser's assessment, 'the differential association theory might be more powerful if it were modified to a "differential identification" of "differential expectation" theory', for while 'the differential association theory stresses the factor of learning, differential identification allows not only for learning but for modification of learning through perceptual processes interacting with personality differences'.[21]

## 'Anomie'—Merton's version

Robert K. Merton, in *Social Theory and Social Structure*, has in some very well-known chapters explored the concept of deviance and made use of Durkheim's original idea of *anomie* in a very special way.[22] Merton's analysis depends first upon accepting the existence of a more or less general and organized system of values controlling the behaviour of the members of any social group, be it large or small; and secondly, on the existence of institutionalized means governing access to culturally defined ends and acceptable social goals. If the accepted means are inadequate and the culturally-prescribed goals are hence unrealizable for large sections of the population, a state of tension and frustration occurs which both individuals and groups have to resolve as best they can, taking, perhaps, clues from the way in which they see that other people are reacting to the frustrating situation. American society, it is argued, opens up before its citizens more or less limitless goals. Everyone with ability, resource and a willingness to work hard can earn a million dollars—this is the often quoted American Dream recently upheld yet again by President Nixon himself, and which has no counterpart in this country. But any society which is achievement-orientated, which stresses the goal of success as an end in itself almost but, of course, not entirely irrespective of the means employed, is exposed to this kind of frustration and strain simply because, as a matter of cold fact, the numbers who are enabled to achieve success must inevitably be severely limited.

But it is not merely lack of opportunity but lack of opportunity within a society which over-values the success and achievement motif that produces this condition of Mertonian *anomie*. In countries of greater poverty and with much more rigid and clearly defined class systems this source of *anomie* would be almost non-existent and so this criminogenic source would be absent too.

Faced with this kind of frustration individuals react in different ways which depend partly, so it would seem reasonable to infer, upon their personality structure and partly upon the specific social situation in which they find themselves. Apart from conformism which implies the acceptance of conventional ends and means and has naturally no criminogenic implications, Merton puts forward four possible kinds of reaction, some of which could have both deviant and delinquent outcomes:

1. Innovation or the acceptance of culturally prescribed ends but the rejection of the conventional means, for example, criminal and deviant behaviour.
2. Ritualism which involves the rejection of cultural ends but the acceptance of institutionalized means, a form of adaptation which requires a somewhat tepid acceptance of things as they are without any irritable striving to change them, in colloquial terms merely going through the motions but without conviction or drive.
3. Retreatism which is a rejection of both prescribed means and ends, resulting in social apathy and a lack of life goals which leaves the individual 'in a social vacuum without direction or meaning'. Perhaps the members of so-called 'problem families' typify this kind of deviant reaction.
4. Rebellion which rejects the *status quo* and culturally prescribed ends and seeks to promote others in their place. 'This pattern', says Merton, 'is exemplified by adolescents teaming up in gangs or becoming part of a youth movement with a distinctive subculture of its own.'

Much of the force of Merton's analysis depends upon how far he is accurate in his suggestion that upward social mobility is usually blocked for lower-class youth and especially, of course, for lower-class males in American society today. We have no real way to answer this question, and must be content with stating it and adding that some social scientists have challenged Merton's pessimism.

One might interject here what is more or less a footnote, but an interesting one, to the present discussion, to say that L. Srole has tried to develop this anomic concept in psychological terms relating to the reaction of the individual himself which he calls *anomia*.[23] His yardstick is a scale divided into five sections indicating the state of mind of an individual who thinks that:

1. The authorities are indifferent to his needs.
2. Little can be achieved in a society where everything is unforeseeable.
3. Individual aims in life fade away instead of being realized.
4. Life has little meaning and has nothing to offer; and
5. There is no one to rely on for moral and social support when in trouble.

Although the sociological concept of anomie is to be thought of as a distinct form of social reality, 'it is reasonable', as Szabo says, 'to assume that individuals suffering from *anomia* are more likely to display deviant behaviour when the social system itself is characterized by *anomie*'.

The position of a society which enjoys an ever increasing level of monetary and material success is likely to become increasingly complicated and bizarre. Just as we now find ourselves obliged to speak of both real deprivation and relative deprivation, so in the criminological field, we seem to be required to think of frustration and relative frustration. And it might well be the case that, even if the barriers against social mobility become more permeable than perhaps they are at present, there will still remain a group of people who are genuinely disadvantaged (the residual poor), and a further group who consider themselves to be disadvantaged *vis-à-vis* other groups with whom they consider themselves to be comparable.

All this, it would seem, tends towards the conclusion that, in so far as social and economic frustrations are capable of producing a kind of criminal backlash effect, crime and similar associated disorders will always be with us unless we undertake a very substantial reorganization of both our social norms and our social institutions—an outcome which is extremely unlikely, however desirable it may appear to some of us on either moral or religious grounds or both.

# Crime and social class 4

While it is generally believed that crime as a whole is outstandingly the preserve of lower-social-class individuals, there are authors who dispute such a statement and who would claim that this is an impression that middle- and upper-class groups are keen to foster. They sometimes go on to argue that middle-class people, who, almost by definition, consist of the white-collar offenders discussed above, are much less likely to be prosecuted, even if found out, for the crimes and delinquencies that they commit than are lower-class offenders. Herman Mannheim speaks of 'a conspicuous lack of information on this subject', and points out that in Britain 'neither criminal statistics nor prison statistics contain anything on it; even such potential indices of class as occupation and educational standard of offenders are not recorded', and we are perforce obliged to rely upon limited and partial studies for data on the connection between social stratification and criminal behaviour.[1] There is no time here to go into the elaborate byways of this complex and sometimes circumlocutory argument, and we could perhaps do no better for our present purpose than to conclude with Terence Morris that 'legally defined delinquency is a social characteristic of the working classes in general and of the unskilled worker in particular'.[2] Morris adds that 'The behaviour of individuals in other social classes is so organized that departure from established norms is far less likely to bring the non-conformist into collision with the criminal law.' Indeed, a fair amount of evidence in support of this view may be obtained from research done in other countries, especially in Europe and in America. Furthermore, a recent and fairly extensive enquiry into the known and the admitted delinquencies of a substantial number of adolescents in this country has shown that there is, in fact, a significant correlation between the social class of juveniles and the number and frequencies of the delinquencies they commit. Dr Lynn McDonald showed that the variable of father's occupation was the one most closely associated with child delinquency and that the chief difference lies between those families at the lowest end of the social class scale and the rest of the population; in other words, the most delinquent children in terms of their own admission and also in terms of their known offences come from households in the unskilled manual worker group.[3]

TABLE 1

*Social class distribution of detected offenders and of all occupied males*

| Social class | 1951 Detected offenders (occupied) and mostly males % | Occupied males (Liverpool C.B.) % | 1961 Detected offenders (occupied) and mostly males % | Occupied males (Liverpool C.B.) % |
|---|---|---|---|---|
| I and II | — | 17 | — | 10 |
| III (Non-manual) | 18 | 16 | 14 | 19 |
| III (Manual) | 21 | 34 | 27 | 37 |
| IV | 20 | 10 | 21 | 18 |
| V | 41 | 22 | 38 | 16 |
| All | 100 | 100 | 100 | 100 |
| No. | (151) | | (205) | |

Source. Liverpool police records.

My own figures giving socio-economic status of adult offenders in Liverpool for all those who were gainfully employed during the years 1951 and 1961 show that a similar picture emerges. It is the manual rather than the non-manual workers groups which evidence the highest incidence of known offences. It is well to remind ourselves, however, that here we are thinking only about those offenders known to the police. These not perhaps very surprising findings are still, of course, open to the criticism that in a class-divided society such as Britain lower-class people will almost inevitably be those whose offences are likely to be picked on for legal action and prosecution. The argument, however, that there are differential arrest rates between the social classes rests upon other foundations and more impressionistic data.

*Middle-class offenders*

In recent years there has been a growing interest in delinquency amongst members of the middle classes in America. While earlier studies tended to concentrate upon the crimes endemic in the typical slum, the delinquencies of the more well-to-do families tended to be overlooked, even denied. One reason for this, one might suppose, is the fact that working-class offences would until recently be regarded as more threatening to the established order than the recklessness of their own youngsters. The recent revolt amongst students and undergraduates may, however, have altered all this, and the fact that it is the more privileged young people who are currently giving most trouble to the authorities (replacing over here, for example, the teddy boys, mods and rockers of earlier years) is causing deep concern among the parental generation.

Some American commentators have suggested that delinquency amongst middle-class American youth is on the increase. In the absence of reliable statistics it is impossible to prove or to disprove such a claim, but a growing volume of self-reported data collected from school children and students indicates that there has always been a fair degree of illegal and deviant behaviour amongst the more favoured social groups. Vaz suggests that 'data are accumulating regularly on the theft, drinking, gambling, and sexual activities of these boys', and he goes on to state that 'automobile offences (which include drag-racing, driving without a licence etc.,) are higher among "white-collar" than "blue-collar" boys'.[4] He suggests there is a hint here of a connection between such manifestations of middle-class delinquency and what David Matza has called the 'subterranean

CRIME AND SOCIAL CLASS

values' of society as a whole—'a disdain for work, search for pleasure, thrills, adventure'—which 'casts some doubt on the protective influence of the middle-class family socialization process'. Moreover, one of the strategies for allaying anxiety is for parents, teachers, social workers and so on to tend to treat a middle-class child who breaks legal and/or social group norms as a 'behaviour problem' rather than as a delinquent, and to react with psychiatric understanding and treatment rather than punitively.

Involvement at any depth with the teenage youth culture is, perhaps likely to lead some youngsters from better-off homes into inadvertent and often unintended delinquencies. It is an illustration of the way in which conformity to the behaviour pattern and norms of a group of peers can be conducive to criminality, comparable in many ways to the corner boy's acceptance of a limited amount of racketeering and dishonesty in order to make himself acceptable to his pals.

In Britain it may well be that in such matters as drug-taking we can see how a similar involvement by middle-class youth in teenage culture can have criminogenic consequences. Participation in protest marches and demonstrations (sometimes, but by no means always, supported for idealistic political reasons) can also lead to violent clashes with the police and to prosecutions for various kinds of offences. At adult level, Marcus has suggested, basing his views on a study of 797 convicted prisoners admitted to Wakefield Prison in the period 1947-8, that there is 'a working-class-middle-class criminality dimension, contrasting thieves and housebreakers at one end with false pretenders and homosexuals at the other'.[5]

Bad social adjustment and inharmonious early home background in a working-class milieu tend to produce chronic thieves and housebreakers, while similar adverse factors in a middle-class milieu seem to result in a passive psychological type likely to commit homosexual or false-pretences offences. Marcus' analysis is extremely interesting even if not entirely conclusive, since his research group was a highly selective one consisting entirely of prisoners.

One of the factors which seems to distinguish between lower- and upper-class offenders is the degree of sophistication and self-control involved (see the typology of offenders on p. 167 below). Many lower-class crimes are impulsive, often crudely carried out, frequently repetitive, employing force, perhaps, as much as skill, and very often directed against other people's tangible property and possessions. By contrast, middle-class offenders seem more adroit at selecting the kind of offence which is difficult to pin down and in choosing the appropriate moment to carry out the crime.

Moreover, when middle-class parents break the law they do so in ways that are unknown to and unavailable to their children and thus they cannot provide the kind of delinquent model that perhaps manual workers may sometimes provide for their offspring. Better-off people are also possibly less tempted by the rewards of petty theft, and more likely to lose their status and income if found out. They experience, then, something of a social disincentive to commit minor delinquencies, although major crime may still appeal to them.[6]

Marcus, in fact, has made the interesting suggestion that 'for each type of criminality there is a different type of "bad" home background' which might well explain such class-based and culturally-distinct differential delinquencies.

Another theory that has been expounded to account for the alleged difference between middle- and working-class children's delinquency has been put forward by Albert Cohen, who seems to have been greatly influenced by the 'masculine protest' theory which Talcott Parsons and others have advanced to explain the aggressiveness of well-favoured American youth.[7] Very simply, this view stems from the judgement that the contemporary American family is female-dominated and that this tends to produce a conflict of role-perception on the part of boys who are in danger of identifying psychologically during the growing-up process with feminine instead of with masculine models. Their reaction to this sensed danger is to exaggerate the more obvious forms of masculinity such as toughness, physical courage, and aggressiveness. So fears of homosexuality and anxieties generated by dread of not being thought a 'proper man' impel middle-class boys, in particular, to demonstrate their manhood by wild, reckless and hence often delinquent behaviour.

There is no easy way to prove or disprove such theories. It is likely, however, that such elements are operating in an unknown number of individual cases, although American culture may in this way be rather different from ours. I would have thought that there is rather less fear of homosexual tendencies in England than in the United States. One piece of evidence is the fact that contemporary pop groups are invariably composed of young males whose appeal, incidentally, does not appear to be confined solely to the female section of the audiences. Laurie says,

> It is curious that the current favourites among the teenagers are almost indistinguishable from girls themselves. Increasingly there tend to be fewer distinctions between the social roles of males and females. The decreasing importance of virility among the boys and the increase of more feminine interests, music, singing and so on, and on occasion *the apparent sexual confusion or indifferent sexuality*, like the *Rolling Stones*, who are sexy but not particularly male, can be seen as an adaptation to the self-assertion of this large group of sub-teenage girls in whom, too, sexuality is not perfectly developed, who resent moreover the traditional man-dominated role prescribed for women, and who demand the freedom to make decisions that boys have.[8]*

## *Ecological approach*

Perhaps the best known of all criminological investigations which sought to uncover the relationship between what we might loosely call the social geography of the city and the location of juvenile delinquents' homes is that carried out in the period between the two world wars by Clifford Shaw and his associate Henry D. McKay.[9] This is usually referred to as the ecological approach and is methodologically greatly indebted to the pioneer work of the famous Chicago school of urban sociologists who, under the impetus of Robert Ezra Park and others, were responsible for developing a zonal concept of urban growth. This idea, which has subsequently proved unviable, depended upon an orderly outward growth of distinct zones radiating from the centre of the city in a series of concentric circles (rather like the growth rings on the trunk of a tree) (see Fig. 3). Shaw claimed that there was a pattern of delinquency associated

* My italics.

with each of the five main urban zones with a fairly steady progression from very high to comparatively low and finally to virtually non-delinquent areas as one travelled from the city centre out to the suburbs and high class bourgeois neighbourhoods. Relying entirely upon records of juvenile court cases or police arrest information, Shaw and McKay showed that in Chicago and in many other large American cities a striking preponderance of young delinquents was invariably to be found in the physically dilapidated and socially depressed 'slum' districts, and especially in what was termed the zone of transition where old property could be adapted to accommodate immigrants and other transients. In some localities, it is claimed, no less than 15 to 25 per cent of the boys aged between ten and seventeen were arrested in any single year. Since each successive year would involve more and more individual boys, it does not seem wildly unfair to refer to such localities as delinquescent or delinquency saturated areas. These zones of transition (sometimes referred to by planners as 'twilight zones') were usually to be found close to localities of an interstitial nature, i.e. areas squashed between industrial and commercial premises, factories, railyards, docks, warehouses. They showed, moreover, that while the total population of such areas changed in the course of time, becoming replaced by a new wave of immigrants and transients, the delinquency rates remained stable. This seemed to imply that certain social influences continued to operate and to imprint themselves upon each fresh wave of inhabitants. Shaw and McKay identified this pervading social influence as 'social disorganisation' by which they meant an absence of community-based efforts to remedy existing defects and to establish a set of stable behaviour norms. This situation shows obvious resemblance to *anomie* although Shaw and McKay do not make use of this concept in their analysis. It further has affinities with Sutherland's differential association theory since it involves amongst other things the continuity of delinquent forms and patterns arising from imitation and interaction with delinquents being transmitted as social traditions to successive generations of children—rather in the way in which street games and songs are handed down. It is not so much a community of individual people that one is thinking about in delinquency areas as a community of ideas, values, attitudes and institutionalized and sometimes delinquent behaviour forms.

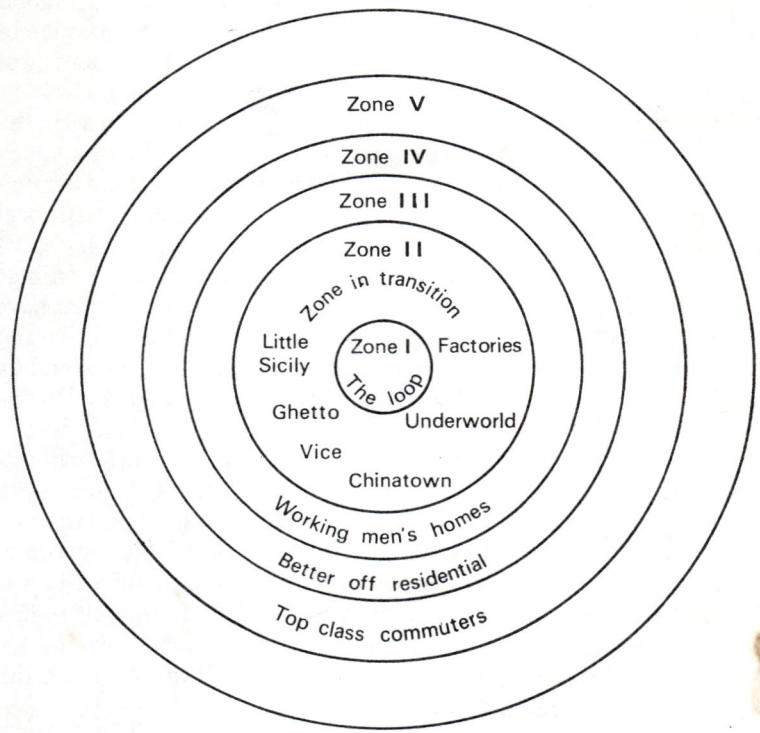

FIGURE 3
*Chicago: zonal growth pattern*

Shaw's work has, in spite of much criticism, proved to have survival-value. Critics have pointed out various inconsistencies in his theories; most notable and telling is the fact that in his zeal to describe symptoms of social disorganization he failed to grasp the significance of distinctive patterns of stable organization. Frederick Thrasher, for example, had already demonstrated in that same city of Chicago only a few years previously that juvenile gangs operated in interstitial localities and he and his fellow workers claimed to have isolated the staggering number of 1,313 separate units in the early nineteen-twenties. Furthermore, the concentric zone theory of urban growth was not found by Lander to hold good for Baltimore where the industries tended to be concentrated in peripheral areas.[11] Shaw and McKay's somewhat naive statistical methods have also come in for criticism.

In Britain and France, for example, it has been found that the 'difficult' housing estate is emerging as a new kind of delinquency area comparable in some ways, such as social class and status-ranking, to the old slum neighbourhood, but resulting from local authority slum clearance policy rather than from the incursion of immigrants. One must not, however, over-emphasize the failings of Shaw and McKay's position nor exaggerate the changes that have overtaken modern societies. Much of value remains in what is, on any assessment, a major empirical work and, as far as lower-class offenders are concerned, their insights and analysis still seem to carry considerable weight.

It is somewhat curious that Dr Mannheim, in his textbook *Comparative Criminology*, elected to consider Shaw's pioneer work on delinquency areas in his section headed 'Non-Class-Oriented Theories' since, although it is true that Shaw seldom drew attention to the notion of social class, the concept is implicit in almost everything that he has to say about crime. I would prefer myself to talk about Shaw and McKay's work as a bridge between a preliminary and very necessary social and delinquent cartographic stage and the subsequent and even more influential stage in which theories based on the notion of the criminal subculture have received the limelight. For the concept of the delinquent subculture has now in recent years most usefully come to supplant the place of the delinquency area in criminological analysis, thus opening up what has proved to be a veritable gold mine for both sociological research and theorizing.

*Subcultural theory: American*

The idea of a delinquency-prone subculture has slowly emerged during the present century until it has now become one of the most influential of all sociological explanations for the existence and character of lower-class criminality and, above all, of the prevalence of juvenile and adolescent gangs which are so frequently referred to in American literature. The concept is one that has been borrowed from anthropology and, as is the way with sociologists, modified and adapted to fit their own purposes and to account for somewhat different data. Sometimes criminologists such as Cohen use the notion of a subculture more as a kind of contraculture, i.e. a form of behaviour which is antagonistic to the values of the society as a whole rather than a variation upon a traditional set of themes. There are two broad streams in the American literature, both of which involve either explicitly or implicitly the notion of a delinquent subculture but which are strikingly contradictory on a number of important points.

Perhaps the best known exponent of the theory of the delinquent subculture as an explanation from one particular point of view for the prevalence and misdeeds of lower-class juvenile gangs is Albert Cohen whose thesis has proved to be most fertile at the theoretical level.

Cohen's analysis owed much to the earlier work of Durkheim and Merton. His work is notable for his rejection of the earlier idea that cultural transmission (i.e. the traditional aspects of delinquency) adequately accounts for the quality of juvenile criminality and its various manifestations. Being a sociologist, he also could not accept that either general psychological or specific psychiatric disabilities could account for the endemic nature of child crime in modern societies. Although he does not deny individual proclivities as contributory factors, he believes that some general sociological influences of a structural nature must be invoked to account adequately for all the known facts. These influences exert their maximum effect when groups of individuals who are occupying similar positions in the social system are brought into close association and so come to evolve identical ways of coping with their common problems. Confronted with the standards and demands of a society which is dominated by middle-class norms and committed to the attainment of middle-class goals, working and lower-class youth (and males most especially) feel acutely frustrated and rejected. They react to this frustration by corporate rejection of the conventional values. At the same time that they are demonstrating their hostility to a denigrating higher-class culture they derive a kind of substitute social status from their own positions within the juvenile gang. Rather as, in schools, some bigger and rather oafish boys, unable to become leaders amongst their peers and to become captains of sport or prize-winners, find an alternative outlet by lording it over an assortment of juniors and, in colloquial language, become 'king of the kids'. Moreover, they probably experience feelings of security and personal worth from their intimate associations within their separate anti-social gangs, which further helps to reinforce their allegiance to non-conformist values and commit them to a delinquent, anti-authority way of life. Some of their group escapades cannot be interpreted in terms of material gains at all. They seem best understood as non-utilitarian and negative (to use Cohen's own terminology) reactions against the rules of society itself. Delinquent acts and acts of vandalism in particular are to be thought of, then, as expressive emotional outlets for children and youths in a social situation where they experience status frustration. This does not, of course, mean that every theft or criminal act is merely to be thought of as a kind of defiance against authority, but that this, in lower-class communities, is their prevailing overall tone and significance. Cohen's young gangsters, in spite of the hedonistic goals they are also said to be pursuing, are much less engaging and pleasant to encounter (at least in print) than the young corner boys and comparatively simple-minded layabouts of the Chicago slums in the time of Frederick Thrasher.

I have said that the American literature offers two distinct types of delinquent subculture of which Cohen epitomizes one variety; Walter B. Miller perfectly exemplifies the other.[10] Miller's perspective is much more anthropological than sociological and, as a result, his description and analysis of lower-class delinquency tends to stress the criminogenic elements in traditional life-patterns associated with low-income and under-privileged social groups in general, rather than developing Cohen's theme of status frustration and inter-class tensions.

Miller argues that delinquency arises in lower-class communities more or less 'naturally' out of the normal way of life. Far from being intent on the achievement goals of bourgeois society, these lower-class youths become delinquent as much by accident as purposefully, simply because their lives are governed by a pattern of values which he calls the 'focal concerns' and because these focal concerns have delinquent overtones.

These focal concerns centring around the need to show toughness and smartness in outwitting one's opponents, the search for excitement, a fatalistic belief in luck, and a stubborn desire to be free of cramping restraints, can all bring the lower-class boy into conflict with the law and with the norms of 'respectable' society. Low-class culture is inured to the concept of 'trouble', which is variously seen as emanating from sexual involvement, from drinking habits, or from hitting across the rules of school and the representatives of the much more powerful middle-class group. 'Trouble' is something you are in constant danger of falling into, an ineluctable concomitant of life in a slum environment, a topic frequently on people's lips, one of the everyday hazards of life that mothers, at any rate, desperately hope and pray that their children will somehow avoid.

*Follow-up studies since Cohen*

Cohen's book led to a considerable amount of work amongst American social scientists following up his clues and hypotheses in greater detail. The most influential of these is undoubtedly Cloward and Ohlin's *Delinquency and Opportunity*.[11] These authors subtitled their book *A Study of Delinquent Gangs*, and it is well to remind ourselves of the fact that what they have to say is about collective and not about individualistic delinquent behaviour. It is also not without significance that they dedicated their work to Robert K. Merton and Edwin H. Sutherland. They were particularly concerned with the different forms of delinquent adaptation that lower-class youths selected as manifestations of their deviance and of their basic economic and status frustration. The kind of delinquent behaviour chosen by adolescent gangs, in their view, depended upon the opportunities or upon the lack of opportunities for deviant conduct that each specific locality could offer. They hypothesized three major types of delinquent subculture which they termed 'criminal', 'conflict' and 'retreatist' respectively. Each is said to be related first, to the 'opportunity structure' of the existing locality, and secondly, to the degree to which youngsters are in touch with, and influenced by, association with older age groups.

The traditional gang literature descriptive of American slum life portrayed children and young people in touch with adult criminals, racketeers, gamblers and others engaged in more or less full-time illicit occupations. The existence of these criminals and racketeers provided models for dissident youth to relate their own behaviour and careers to, and was thus a fruitful source of delinquent motivation filtering down the generations. This portrays *par excellence* the ideal criminal sub-culture.

But Cloward and Ohlin note that juvenile delinquents are nowadays much less in contact with adult criminals. For one thing, some lower-class neighbourhoods lack a sufficient degree of cohesiveness to make social contact between the age groups a viable possibility. Rehousing schemes and public welfare policies have further helped them to break up the pattern of slum neighbourhoods and to make them unattractive to adult gangsters and racketeers. Disadvantaged youths in such localities are hence deprived both of legitimate and of illegitimate avenues for achieving status and other social rewards. In such circumstances, they tend to solve their adjustment problems by resorting to violence. Achievement values are in such terms as 'rep' and 'heart' and in not being 'chicken', and conflict for conflict's sake either between police and gangs or between the rival gangs themselves becomes the order of the day. It is also extremely interesting to note Cloward and Ohlin's suggestion that the presence of detached social workers could actually increase the amount of violence for the paradoxical reason that, because youths seemed to interpret having a street-club worker attached to them as 'an act of social deference', gangs in time 'came to compete for the prestigeful symbol'.

The 'retreatist' subculture, on the other hand, seems to attract the failures and drop-outs from all organized groups, including those who could not sustain successful membership of either delinquent or conflict gangs. Retreatist youth tends to withdraw into a private and inverted twilight world where, in association with other 'hipsters', they pursue individual 'kicks' in the form of narcotics, alcohol and uninhibited sexuality.

The various theories outlined above are all in process of empirical testing. Irving Spergel's *Racketville, Slumtown and Haulberg*, as its title suggests, is an application of Cloward and Ohlin's analysis to the city of New York.[12] Spergel's research largely vindicated the Cloward and Ohlin theory. He claimed to have found evidence of three distinctive types of neighbourhood each with its special kind of delinquent subculture. Racketville corresponded to an area in New York where juvenile delinquency was highly integrated with adult crime. Slumtown, another neighbourhood, contained youngsters with relatively low aspirations and expectations committed to a physically violent way of life. Haulberg was intermediate between the other two areas, characterized at times by resentment against superior social groups and classes but with some access to legitimate opportunities. The retreatist drug-addict subculture did not emerge with any great clarity as being associated with any specific kind of neighbourhood, although the conflict area seemed to have more drug users than the others. The rackets' subculture existed in a neighbourhood with a predominantly Italian population, while the conflict subculture was in an extremely blighted and socially degraded slum occupied by considerable numbers of Puerto Rican immigrants. The largely theft subculture was located in an area of mixed European nationalities who seemed to place considerable emphasis on material goods and possessions, but with integration between age groups confined to older and younger children and youths, and with few, if any, connections with adult groups.

Martin Gold's study of the town of Flint derived its orientation mainly from Cohen.[13] Flint, a medium sized town of some 200,000 people, is dominated by General Motors, lying as it does some fifty miles north of Detroit, and seems to possess no real down-town slum area such as earlier criminologists had concentrated upon. Gold's core sample of twelve-year-old delinquents consisted of 229 boys, their fathers and mothers, who were all interviewed. Negroes were excluded, as were children with I.Qs. below 79. The whole group was divided into 'repeaters' and 'sometime' delinquents, and a control group of non-delinquents with similar backgrounds was drawn for comparative purposes from public school files. A number of conventional ideas about low status and delinquency were explored. It seems, on the basis of the Flint evidence at any rate, that quality of educational and recreational provision does not adequately explain the well-known connection between the two. At most we can assume that neighbourhoods which offer poor facilities are generally less attractive, and also that they provide handy targets for aggressiveness. The nature of family life and relationships seems to be much more crucial. Repeaters seem to be less attracted to their own families than the non-delinquents. They have much less to do with their parents and discuss personal problems with their parents less frequently; all of which implies that the family is failing to set and apply socially accepted conduct norms. Above all, 'attraction and control in father-son relationships' was found to be more crucial than mother-son relationships in producing child delinquency. Delinquents were much more vulnerable to personal failure at school and hence came to experience status problems in their later working lives which could account for their hostility towards society at large. At the same time, Gold effectively tried to explain higher-class boys' delinquencies by the same theory, although, in their case, it was clear that the risk of failure and frustration was greatly reduced. Thus we are led to conclude that delinquency is the ideal solution for status problems for members of all social classes, because, as Cohen had earlier pointed out, it simultaneously cocks a firm snook at the frustrating society and also offers opportunities for earning status by deeds of daring amongst the serried ranks of fellow dissidents. Gold's final analysis, therefore, is strongly supportive of Cohen and a firm rejection of Miller's position, although it can by no means be thought of as more than a small-scale exploratory investigation.

One further American research project can also be discussed here since it has considerable bearing upon the main problem of the extent to which lower-class youths are in fact reacting aggressively against the norms and goals of the predominating culture. If it can be shown, for instance, that working-class boys accept the validity of the goals of middle-class society, even though they themselves assess their chances of attaining these goals to be slender, the Cohen theory of a positive and hostile rejection cannot be sustained and a good deal of the force of the latter's analysis evaporates.

Short and Strodtbeck deal with the theoretical issues involved in Chicago's Y.M.C.A. detached-worker programme, and offer an extremely complex statement which can best be thought of as merely an interim report on a research venture still far from completed.[14] Methodologically, some very interesting techniques were employed, notably an exploratory attempt to obtain youngsters' self-evaluation by means of a paired comparison instrument (a semantic differential test) administered in the field to both delinquent and non-delinquent white and coloured boys. The major result was that they found that the earlier theories of Cohen, Cloward and Ohlin and Miller were only partially viable. The subcultural juvenile delinquency here examined does not represent a reaction against superior-class society *nor does it involve a wholesale repudiation of middle-class norms.* It is merely that in the absence of any structured way for achieving the values institutionalized and highly regarded by superior social groups, something which the authors call 'a kind of vacuum' is created which the youngsters occupy with 'time-filling expenditures of energy built around capacities for gratification through interaction with the gang'. Or, in simpler language, they waste their time and energies on dress, dances, fights and delinquencies which have no relevance to the wider social world of work and maturity for which middle-class youths are being rather more carefully groomed by their parents and teachers. Even if the latter are temporarily estranged by excessive involvement in their own youth culture, to the detriment of serious adult-orientated interests, the estrangement is only short-lived and in any case is more apparent than real, since, as Matza and others have argued, there is a strong invisible subterranean link between middle-class youth culture and middle-class adult culture.[15] Working-class boys, however, and those at the bottom of the social pile are likely to become permanently alienated from 'respectable' society. Left to their own resources they mill madly around indulging in delinquencies which effectively set them apart from the wider community. Much of this analysis is based on Negro gangs who appear destined to become lasting social outcasts with all that that implies for future cultural and class divisions.

The vital fact that emerges from Short and Strodtbeck's rather tortuous book is that middle-class prescriptive norms are upheld, to varying degrees, in most social strata which suggests a significant moderation of the more extreme pictures drawn by Cohen and by Cloward and Ohlin. Their position, as far as one can assess it at present, is something of a compromise and amalgam between the views of several earlier research workers and social theorists. Although the last word on delinquent subculture has not yet been written, at least we are beginning to see that the true picture is far from being capable of representation in terms of the simple blacks and whites of the more extreme explanations. Subcultures, like other parts of the social system, are both more complicated and less clearly delineated than some theorists would have us believe.

A study of New York gangs by Lewis Yablonsky shows the same complexity and fluidity already noted in relation to delinquent sub-cultures.[16] The old idea of the closely structured gang with its hierarchy of authority and its definitive roles of leader, lieutenant and follower, as a distinct sociological unit appears to be giving way to the concept of another and much more deadly kind of gang which appears to emerge more or less spontaneously and to be loosely structured around a central core of seriously disturbed members. It is concerned with violence of a somewhat paranoid kind more or less as a form of self-protection. Perhaps its members represent the extreme of Cloward and Ohlin 'boppers' involved in inter-gang combat in an almost hysterical way. It is, perhaps, fortunate that such violent gangs are not highly integrated, otherwise their threat to public order would be very much greater. But, in the conditions of the modern slum, boys with defective personalities can make use of the gang, or, as Yablonsky more often calls it, the 'near-group', for their own essentially asocialized self-expression in organized deviance. The work of the New York City Youth Board has come into being during the past decade precisely to meet the menace presented by such gangs and to find ways of coping with their influence in the form of substitute outlets and ameliorative programmes.

## Delinquency and drift

The discussion about the delinquent subculture rumbles on and every now and again a writer adds a contribution which fills out an earlier insight or modifies the general picture. One of the most influential, and from some points of view most important, of these later contributions comes from David Matza whose *Delinquency and Drift*[17] although published somewhat earlier than Short and Strodtbeck's book does seem to merit individual consideration since it propounds a point of view which to some extent challenges the original formulations of Cohen and other American authorities. Matza is at pains to disassociate himself from positivist assumptions which underlie most modern aetiological theories. 'The subculture of delinquency' as he prefers to call it, rather than 'the delinquent subculture', is not to be thought of as being in direct confrontation with an adult wider community culture as a kind of opposing well-articulated system. The wider culture is, after all, many-sided rather than uniform, and the alleged barriers dividing the two are highly permeable and shifting. Delinquency, radicalism and bohemianism already exist as 'subterranean traditions' even in law-abiding sections of the community who often seem to accept, and even, at times, perhaps, to enjoy vicariously, some allegedly deviant forms of youthful behaviour. Such a view is reminiscent of one which we have touched on earlier which suggests that delinquents are in some sense necessary in order to promote general solidarity. One might go one stage further and suggest that such a view also seems to imply that by contemplating the deviance and delinquencies of others we can in some way release in the safer form of fantasy our own secret and sinister impulses.

Matza asserts that young delinquents use neutralization techniques to soothe their consciences: arguments such as 'everybody does it' or 'nobody got hurt' or 'they wouldn't miss them'. This psychological technique, Matza says, puts the delinquent 'in drift'. That is to say he may commit an offence or he may not. It all depends on the circumstances. It is all a matter of luck. The young delinquent's surrounding subculture 'is simply too rich in options, too poorly delineated and specified, too ambivalent about its enterprises to yield anything approaching clear-cut directives to action'. The difference, then, between the subcultural delinquent and other boys is more apparent than real; at most it is marginal, and the lawbreaking is not intentional. Social workers, Matza avers, tend, unconsciously of course!, to conspire with the young delinquent's viewpoint, thereby reinforcing the neutralization of guilt process. 'It confirms his conception of irresponsibility, and it feeds his sense of injustice. Both support the processes by which the moral bind of law is neutralized. Both facilitate the drift into delinquency.'

## Delinquent subcultures in Britain

Sociological explanations of juvenile crime in this country have followed the Miller rather than the Cohen-Cloward-and-Ohlin lines of analysis. In the main, British researchers and writers have been more empirically oriented than theoretically rich, and their work has tended to be pragmatic and localized. The first name in a line which has become much expanded in recent years is that of Sir Cyril Burt, whose classic study of young delinquents in London is now over forty years old and is still far from being outmoded.[17] Broadly speaking, Burt found that his high delinquency areas were more or less the same as the poverty areas which Charles Booth had described at the end of the previous century. Burt, orientated mainly by psychological knowledge but by no means blind to the influence of social conditions, was one of the first to advance the 'multiple determination' theory which is still more or less the modern orthodoxy. Among his long list of causal factors he places adverse environment outside the home (such as bad street companions and lack of facilities for amusement) eleventh out of his first fifteen major items. 'Defective discipline' is placed first, followed by 'specific instincts', 'general emotional instability', 'morbid emotional conditions', with 'defective family relationships'—specified as 'the absence of a father, the presence of a step-mother'—occupying tenth place. However, the emphasis he places on environmental influence, both inside and outside the home, and the stress he places on the idea of delinquency as essentially learned behaviour have had considerable influence upon later research workers.

The essence of my own Liverpool enquiry, which was based upon detailed interviews with some eighty youth club members, was to suggest that some kinds of delinquency were the norm, even amongst boys who were clearly not basically anti-social in character.[19] No less than thirty of the eighty had in fact appeared before the courts; twenty-two others would have been prosecuted had they been caught; thirteen admitted to any minor peccadilloes such as lorry-skipping, leaving only a dozen or so with untarnished records. Although no psychological tests were made (a defect that later critics seized upon) I considered that the vast majority of my research group (apart from one who seemed to have committed his crimes in order to be 'put away') were far from being maladjusted. In fact I described the delinquencies of the great majority as being 'not so much a symptom of maladjustment as of adjustment to a subculture in conflict with the culture of the city as a whole'. This to the best of my knowledge is the first reference, in British literature at least, in which the notion of subculture is invoked to account for juvenile crime, although the idea was not at that time worked out in any theoretical detail. Nor did I then consider that this juvenile subculture was a conscious rebellion against middle-class society and its values so much as an alternative, tougher working-class way of life in its own right which developed criminalistic aspects more or less fortuitously. It seemed to me that excessive leisure time, the absence of adequate parental models and care, the presence of known adult offenders in the locality together with boys' own natural desire to test themselves in acts of daring, bravado and danger, were a sufficient explanation for delinquent behaviour which invariably tapered off after leaving school and was almost certainly phasic in character. Social conditions and changes may, of course, have altered the cultural life of the dockland very considerably, and it may possibly be a fact that today similarly placed boys who kick over the traces do so more in line with the Cohen thesis as a positive reaction and repudiation of middle-class values and institutions. I have no real way of knowing but recent researches in London do not suggest that we have yet reproduced in this country the acute forms of criminal contracultures which apparently afflict society in the U.S.A.

Professor Sprott and his collaborators at the University of Nottingham were working along similar but distinct lines at the same time.[20] Their study of the Midland mining township of Radby revealed that working-class areas, apparently economically and socially homogeneous, nevertheless were not uniformly crime-prone. They discovered, in fact, that there were two major types of family life which were associated with different but nearby streets. In one, to which the label of Dyke Street was attached, we find a collection of households where a pattern of life has apparently developed over the years which is conducive to delinquency and tolerant of other aberrant forms of behaviour. Round the corner, on the other hand, we find Gladstone Road where a much different and much more bourgeois pattern prevails and where there were in fact no offenders.

The report, which was published privately in 1954, *The Social Background of Delinquency*, dichotomizes the two polar types of street and family background in a most useful way. From it we can see that in a great many respects the so-called 'Black' streets contrasted diametrically with the 'White' streets, although the authors did not find any differences at the employment level (e.g. between skilled and unskilled fathers) to account for the differential delinquency rates.

| *Black* (Dyke Street) | *White* (Gladstone Road) |
| --- | --- |
| Wider household and kinship group, even if not always living together | Nuclear family units |
| Maternal concern alone for welfare and behaviour of children | Concern of both parents |
| Children treated less as children than as little adults to be given as much of their way as possible | Children receive special treatment appropriate with their age |

| *Black* (Dyke Street) | *White* (Gladstone Road) |
|---|---|
| Children taught to be anti-police | Children taught that the police are there to offer help |
| Irregular attendance at Sunday school | Regular attendance at Sunday school |
| Loose sexual codes | Sexual code fairly rigid and middle-class |
| Physical force used to solve problems | Physical force only used as a last resort |
| Children allowed to be aggressive | Children's aggression restrained |
| Houses and possessions kept indifferently | House-pride and enjoyment of garden |
| Stealing only regarded as such when it assumes fair proportions | General respect and care for all property |
| Gamble regularly | Gamble seldom |
| Conscious of a hard past and determined to see their children don't suffer as they did (for example 'If I refuse them it upsets me' attitude) | Made more careful by past memories of hardship |
| Some adult offenders in families and a fair number of juvenile delinquents. Little shame over prison or approved school orders | No offenders or delinquents |
| Street parties. 'Neighbouring' indulged in, but no belief in need to restrain one another | No street parties or 'neighbouring' |

What is hypothesized above is really a kind of rough/respectable dichotomy such as has been described in various community studies and which seems to show that there are two broad strata in any working-class community: those who accept and uphold middle-class norms, and those who do not and who have their own divergent, and sometimes deviant, values and modes of behaving. In a small mining town like Radby it may be possible for the respectables to obtain accommodation side by side in specific streets. In the conditions of a large industrial city it may often not be possible and so in the Liverpool dockland or in the east end of London, roughs and respectables may be obliged to live in closer proximity than either of them like or wish. The fact remains that there is a delinquency-prone section of lower-class population and that in Britain this probably consists partly in reaction against middle-class values and the frustrations imposed by 'Them' against 'Us', and partly in an alternative pattern of life which to some extent exists in its own right.

A stimulating and less wellknown study of delinquency in Exeter showed, for instance, that 41 per cent of the juvenile delinquents lived in a single ward almost entirely consisting of an out-of-town council estate built in the nineteen-thirties.[21] The author of the enquiry report accounted for this by:

1. lack of occupational opportunity; and
2. anti-social norms transmitted from generation to generation; and
3. absence of an adequate remedial and compensatory youth service.

T. P. Morris's wellknown ecological study of Croydon also deals with the fact that delinquency areas existed in certain specific parts of the borough.[22] Having shown that lower-class localities had the highest known crime rates, Morris goes on to account for this in terms similar to my own and to Miller's. He believes that the historic divisions between middle class and working class have produced two typical and distinctive ways of life as alternative, rather than as opposed, cultures. The socialization of middle-class children is geared to the pursuit of long-term goals rather than short-term rewards. They are given standards and expected to adhere to them, and their upbringing in school and home is carried out on a rational and demanding basis. The working-class child whose father is in unskilled employment is much less accustomed to restraint, more attuned to the pleasures of the immediate moment, and apt to resort to force rather than to reason when confronted with any kind of a problem. He is extremely touchy and irritable and is thus much more likely to react by delinquent and other forbidden forms of behaviour.

Peter Willmott's *Adolescent Boys of East London* [23] perpetuates the *Growing Up in the City* story in a not dissimilar geographical context. Instead of the over-publicized 'delinquent generation' composed of countless 'insecure offenders' as Fyvel termed them, Willmott observed young Bethnal Greeners behaving more or less normally. There was, of course, the occasional affray in the streets, common vandalism directed against windows and telephone kiosks, wide spread petty larceny and one somewhat dramatic gang rape of a rather more sinister nature in Victoria Park. The wellknown problems are once more documented: problems, that is to say, of rebelliousness, social frustration, anti-school attitudes, of gang mentality and class consciousness and of modes and norms which are foreign to middle-class cultures. These boys don't want to speak posh, to take part in social play-acting or in any way to seem different from their pals. They opt out of the conventional scholastic rat race, although some, a minority, do cut themselves off from their peers and seek to climb the career ladder into suburbia. But the majority seem more or less satisfied with their way of life—at least while they're young—and if this involves joining in petty crime, rowdiness and destructiveness, the greater the fun and the sense of togetherness. 'It seems probable,' Willmott concludes on the basis of his interviews and observations, 'that something like one Bethnal Green boy in three may appear in court before his twenty-first birthday.'

Dr David Downes also went to the east end of London for his later researches into juvenile crime.[24] He was interested to see how far the accepted subcultural theories propounded by American social scientists were viable in English urban society. Downes is at pains to point out that there are in practice two rather distinct definitions of what constitutes a subculture: one which treats it as being *outside* the context of the dominant culture altogether, and the other that treats it as a negative or positive response to the demands and pressures *inside* the dominant culture. The former produces a kind of co-existence, the latter in its negative aspect can result in lawbreaking and pathological deviance. In the literature there has been some confusion of these two kinds of subculture and nowhere is this more noticeable than in writing about gangs. Dr Downes's findings, which can only be briefly touched upon here, lend little or no support to Cloward and Ohlin's analysis and even less to Cohen's more imprecise formulations. In this country there is as yet no evidence that structured juvenile gangs exist.* The occasional street forays are short-lived and hardly organized, but the most substantial fact which at the moment seems to be 'militating against the emergence of "criminal" subcultures in England is the relative absence of any demonstrably successful "illegitimate opportunity structure"'.

My own view supports Downes's position but one must add that one is talking as always in sociological research about a situation which obtained yesterday. Society changes quickly as new moods and trends emerge and sweep across the country, for example, the phenomenon of student revolt in 1968. But my judgement is that there is much less pressure to achieve in British society via the legitimate opportunity structure also. These two factors seem to combine to produce a much more stable, less ambition-tormented youthful population than apparently exists in the U.S.A. 'The English corner boy', to quote Downes, 'successfully traverses the humiliations of school and job allocation by his re-affirmation of his traditional working-class values.' He also, one might add, in the comparative affluence of contemporary society, makes up for what he otherwise lacks in the sphere of leisure and recreation.

But as we have already indicated earlier, there are some signs that adult criminal gangs may be on the increase in this country. Protection rackets centring around organized gambling, especially in the London area, and occasional outbursts of violence, even of killings, associated with these gambling protection gangs, as, for example, in the *Blind Beggar* affair,† are indicators that the winds of crime can change quite fast. What, however, remains to be shown is that there is any connection between adult criminals and juvenile delinquents on any planned organized basis other than on casual contact.

A more recent sociocultural enquiry by Mrs Elton Mayo which contrasts and compares delinquency areas in Marseille and Wrexham

* Gangs in certain parts of down-town Glasgow have been persistently reported in the national press in recent years and they may well constitute an exception to this generalization but it is not yet certain how far they are formally structured. For confirmation of this see J. Patrick, *A Glasgow Gang Observed*, Eyre Methuen, 1973.

† Readers may recall this as a public house in which a shooting occurred during the events which led up to what we now know as the Kray brothers case in London.

suggests that although the Queen's Park area of the latter is clearly criminogenic there is no tie up between the juvenile and adult delinquent systems.[25] In Marseille on the other hand, there is such a tie up and the prognosis for most young offenders there is accordingly much more pessimistic. Mrs Mayo's findings may be related to an earlier study of both adult and juvenile crime in Glasgow carried out by John Mack,[26] who suggests that adult offenders of the professional type tend nowadays to live in socially neutral areas rather than in the deteriorated slums, and to retain contact with other professionals by means of a loose network of connections which are mainly activated at irregular intervals when 'jobs' are being planned or undertaken. If this is so, then it adds further support to the idea that juvenile and adult delinquent structures do not interact either geographically or organizationally. A great deal of research, however, still needs to be done on this aspect of our changing social structure and its related delinquency structure.

An ethnographic study by Howard Parker[27] of young people growing up in a socially disadvantaged area of inner Liverpool has recently shown how delinquent boys adapt their behaviour in dynamic interaction with the neighbourhood and its changing opportunities for theft and excitement. Parker has noted many continuities with earlier subcultural studies but he stresses that the process is much more interactive and complex than some investigators have supposed, and that the delinquent activities of lower-working-class boys in down-town areas take place within a constantly shifting matrix, including the reactions of the police and other authority figures, which makes it difficult for an outsider to predict possible future manifestations.

# The socialization process and crime 5

Socio-cultural interpretations of the nature and meaning of crime and delinquency, it will be clear, imply that for delinquents the socialization process has in some significant respects broken down. While the family must be regarded as the primary source of ethical values and social attitudes, especially in the upper and middle classes, the school is an important secondary institution which, as we shall see, has a vital contribution to make both to delinquency causation and delinquency prevention.

## Delinquency and family failure

It is pre-eminently within the family circle that the growing child learns about the rights and needs of others and how to adjust his own egocentric behaviour to the realities of a social group. Even more important are the emotional ties with the parents. A great deal of psychological and psychiatric research has been concentrated on the focus of maternal affection and the effects which its absence or impairment have for the personality structure of the child. Dr Lee Robins sums up a widely held point of view in psychological circles when she wrote in her study which followed the after-careers of some 500 ex-attenders at child guidance clinics over a thirty year period that 'comparison of the siblings of various diagnostic groups has shown that the behaviour problems found in the sociopathic group seem to be *familial* . . . their parents as well as their siblings have a high rate of occupational failure, marital discord, arrests and drinking'.[1] So the disturbed and delinquent family often produces the disturbed and delinquent children. And this applies to all social classes and to all income groups, although, as we know, the upper-

and middle-class parents are much more successful than lower-class parents in getting their children's misbehaviour dealt with as a psychiatric problem rather than as a criminal offence.

Children require sound discipline as Burt long ago pointed out, and this kind of discipline has at least two components: one, affection; and two, control. Control needs to be consistent and reliable if it is to contribute to a sound and stable character structure. If punishment is to be resorted to, it must be of a consistent and predictable nature. The temporary disturbance of the normally loving relationship between parent and child is usually sufficient in most cases to give the child the necessary jolt and to establish appropriate guidelines for his conduct. Given a relationship based on mutual affection and trust the child will respond to his parent's anger or grief by inhibiting the behaviour which produced such a reaction; and, conversely, he will tend to reproduce the kind of behaviour which produces the warm, supportive parental concern.

It is, in fact, only when something goes wrong with the parent-child relationship, or when the social environment is grossly criminogenic, that serious delinquency is likely to eventuate. There are often thought to be two kinds of family upset which are conducive to delinquency: one is the broken home and the other, a derivative of this, mothers going out to work. We will consider them both rather briefly here in order to get them into a proper perspective. The broken-home theory is now largely discredited both in psychological and sociological literature. Dr Lee Robins concluded on the basis of her very careful analysis that 'a broken home which does not involve parental discord does not lead to adult anti-social behaviour'. It is now generally realized that the absence of one parent or the other, while causing some inevitable imbalance in the structure, cannot result in child delinquency unless it is also symptomatic and the result of some deeper emotional disturbance and rupture in the pattern of normal family relationships. If this were not so, then almost every offspring of a widow or a widower would become a delinquent, as in fact does not happen.

The idea that mothers going out to work leads to neglect of the children and so increases their risk of becoming delinquents is also unsupported by scientific research. Barbara Wootton looked at the evidence and dismissed it as unproven.[2] On the other hand, Ivan Nye thought that there was a slight association, probably because of a reduction in supervision, between mothers at work and children's delinquent behaviour.[3] We may, perhaps, conclude that fulltime-working mothers of families which are undergoing any kind of stress or unusual difficulty might conceivably neglect their children to such a degree that their children could fall foul of the law but that, by and large, no ill effects would occur in stable families where interpersonal relationships are sound and warm.

Furthermore, Simon Yudkin and Anthea Holme, who have had a chance to look at the literature that has been published since Barbara Wootton, are not inclined to attach much significance to the contribution that mothers in employment can make to the incidence of child delinquency.[4]

The Gluecks believe that individual differences of temperament and physical constitution must explain why one child becomes an offender while another one masters his problems or expresses his tensions in more socially acceptable ways. Certain factors in the family environment are especially criminogenic, and they claim to show, on the basis of a very detailed and careful analysis of 500 institutionalized delinquents and a similar number of non-delinquent controls, that it is coincidence of environmental factors acting selectively upon certain personality traits which produces the delinquency.[5] For instance, in their earlier research they discovered that a significantly higher proportion of boys whose fathers were unacceptable models to emulate were to be found among the delinquent group. Dr Andry,[6] Nye[7] and others had also pointed out the importance of the father in the aetiology of delinquency, noting that, when fathers failed to do their task properly or rejected their children, the delinquency risk was greatly increased. But the Gluecks seem to have taken the argument a stage further by showing that the impact of such deprivation is more serious amongst boys characterized by traits of *stubbornness and/or uninhibited motor responses to stimuli and/or acquisitiveness*, all of which are closely linked to bodily constitution. Such information has clear remedial directives. If stubbornness, for example, is innate, no attempt should be made to reduce the trait by direct modification; rather should the re-educator try to guide the boy into socially acceptable and harmless ways of expressing this characteristic.

There is perhaps a useful clue here to understanding particular manifestations of what is often termed the adolescent revolt and which, in certain aspects, has a clear delinquent consequence in cases where youths take part in violent street demonstrations and similar illegal forays solely for the sake of the excitement engendered. We often think of such youths, or at least of those most given to participation in such riotous demonstrations, as being essentially alienated from the mainstream of the culture. Or we think of them as being seriously cut off and dissociated from their families and kindred authority-figures. It may well be the case that revolt and manifest demonstrations of revolt also meet personality needs amongst the ringleaders themselves and that, in terms of the Gluecks' analysis, their stubbornness and lack of inhibitions have not been coped with satisfactorily either by their families, by their schools or by other educative institutions. One would, of course, want to make a sharp distinction here between demonstrations that are genuinely political in origin and which are provoked by the intransigence of authoritarian regimes, and those which are simply the outcome of irritability and hysteria.

## Problem families

The ascription of the adjective 'problem' to certain failing families is an offshoot of social work practice. Since the indices are much in doubt, it is difficult to know whether a delinquent component is an associated aspect of problem status or not. But, taking a problem family to be one which is characterized by child-neglect and which is seen by social workers to be functioning inadequately at various vital levels, Harriet Wilson showed that in Cardiff a case could be made out to suggest that such families' pattern of living did in fact generate juvenile delinquency.[8] Not only did these selected families have a delinquency rate eight times in excess of the city as a whole, but, further, she showed that such families living in relative isolation in low delinquency areas had a delinquency rate similar to those problem families located in the high delinquency areas nearer the city centre. In the case of the children there was clearly a breakdown of culture illustrated by material deprivation and simultaneously by isolation and emotional insecurity. Such children when they become delinquent are clearly not doing so as a result of the social infection of a delinquent subculture or at the instigation of a criminal gang. They become delinquent because the pattern of their family life has chronically broken down, and indeed they often appear not to know that their delinquent acts are in any sense wrong. They are far from being the 'socialized' delinquents of Thrasher, Morris, Miller *et al.*, but the 'unsocialized' and psychologically damaged who have to some extent experienced parental neglect, emotional unfulfilment and exposure to delinquent drift.

*Delinquency and the school*

It was Sir Cyril Burt, I think, who first pointed out that 'The mental and moral harm that an uncongenial occupation works upon older youths may with younger children be effected by an uncongenial education.'[9] He went on to say that 'it is the great weakness of most schools that they so seldom trouble to analyse the reasons for their failure', and asked 'Why is it that the school is not blamed for a child's delinquency more frequently than his home?'—a question that must have fluttered the pedagogical dovecotes at the time it was posed. Burt is thus again revealed as a perceptive pioneer of more recent research work which has shown how the schools themselves, by their internal selective methods and similar authoritarian and divisive procedures, precipitate a certain amount of rebellion and delinquency. John Webb gave a model description of what he called a 'Black' secondary modern school in which he showed how rule-breaking in school can easily lead on to law-breaking outside.[10] Such a school based on the idea of a kind of war between staff and pupils produces a 'blackboard jungle' tradition which can only be eliminated by radical structural changes in organization and a new spirit of determined goodwill emanating from the headteacher downwards. Sir Alec Clegg has described such a process in his own West Riding area where a downtown school of the 'Black' type, with a very high delinquency rate and other associated social problems, was transformed in a very short space of time by a new headmaster with a new policy.[11] Clegg's enquiry was designed to see what relationship severity of caning in school had with the incidence of pupil delinquency. He showed that, in contrast with what might be considered to be the popular view, behaviour was best amongst children who attended school where caning was lightest, and that this finding, moreover, was as valid for the poorer-class as for the middle-class district. In broad terms, in schools where resort to corporal punishment is minimal, delinquency and other indices of disturbance are greatly reduced *irrespective of the social type of locality*—a view that reinforces the old idea that a 'good' school can civilize a whole neighbourhood.

More recently David Hargreaves has produced a study of the social relations and organizational structure of a secondary modern school in a Lancashire city which illustrates in considerable detail and richness of data how the school tended to produce and reinforce its own deviance and delinquency.[12] He showed how, as a result of separating the sheep from the goats, the more able from the less able scholars, and by rewarding the conformists and rejecting the non-conformists, the school created two quite distinctive subcultural groups which emerged into open hostility at the end of their fourth year. By rejecting the academic values of the school the non-conforming 'D' streams achieved informal status within the delinquescent group, a process which the attitude of the teaching staff subconsciously connived at by favouring those who adopted the school's values and formal status-system of captains and similar school-centred awards. The non-conforming boys hence reacted rather like Cohen's gang members by creating their own kind of contra-culture in which delinquency was one form of behaviour which made for acceptance by the group and, at the same time, provided an opportunity for affronting all authority. Hargreaves concluded that:

The implication of much of this analysis is that there is a real sense in which the school can be regarded as a generating factor of delinquency. Although the aims and efforts of the teachers are directed towards deleting such tendencies, the organization of the school and its influence on subcultural development unintentionally foster delinquent values.

To some extent, then, we may say that Hargreaves has shown the sociological and socio-psychological realities and structures which underlie the findings of the West Riding Survey. The two researches are mutually supportive. Furthermore, evidence continues to come in from a study made by the Social Medicine Research Unit of a group of London boroughs that some schools there do seem to exert this kind of criminogenic effect on their less successful pupils. Commenting on the fact that some schools in high delinquency areas have comparatively low rates while others in comparatively low delinquency areas have high ones, the research workers suggest that some schools are effective in protecting their pupils from delinquency risk while other schools are exposing their pupils to just such a risk.[13] The evidence on this issue is admittedly sketchy and as yet inconclusive, but there are grounds for believing that further researches along similar lines to that carried out by David Hargreaves, but over a much more extensive field, could produce some very interesting evidence of great relevance for delinquency prevention. There is undoubtedly something of high aetiological importance in that complex formed by educational experience on the one hand, and job expectation and its associated prospects and status on the other, to which close attention will need to be paid in the future. As Downes has argued, the only way in which the stifled working class adolescent can escape from the 'school-work *status quo*' is by greater political awareness 'which is ultimately the only alternative to delinquency, in the phase of non-attachment preceding home-centredness and the channelling of his aspirations into family life'.[14] Both achievement means and achievement goals need to be restructured if working-class youth is ever to be liberated from the chains of cultural bondage and social inferiority—and the only effective way to bring this about is to make education more realistic and rewarding and the prospect of a skilled job so much more attainable.

## Adult offenders

Much of the foregoing analysis applies equally to adult and to juvenile offenders but we ought to make it clear that there are a number of adult offenders who have no history of juvenile delinquency so far as we know. There are some critical differences between the old and the young in regard to crime. For example, many more older people seem to drift into a habitual kind of criminality more as a result of their own physical and psychological deficiencies than would be true of children. There is a proportion of adults, also, who commit crimes, sometimes isolated offences, because of peculiar temptations. Some white-collar criminals will be numbered among such offenders. Further, there is a group who are committed to crime as a way of life—the professionals, who, though small in numbers, account for a high proportion of the more serious and more successful crimes against property (see the typology of offenders on p. 167 below). But the typical habituated adult offender is an obviously inadequate personality, chronically down on his luck, adrift in society with few, if any, stable personal relationships. His criminality as well as being the end-product of his own personal defects can also fairly enough be partly accounted for in terms of the failure of society to give such alienated individuals the opportunities for the social rehabilitation they so desperately require but have so little will to grasp.

Chronic recidivists of a somewhat low-grade type drift in and out of prisons and similar institutions almost throughout their lives. Tony Parker's *Unknown Citizen* is a typical example of a man who, at the age of fifty, had eight convictions for larceny, storebreaking and housebreaking, had spent a total of twenty-six years in prisons and institutions with an average period of freedom between sentences of only eleven weeks. Yet the total value of all his thefts amounted to a mere £178![15]

Something like twenty-five per cent of all offenders are persistent in their criminal behaviour—the hard core of the recidivist crime problem—and remain to baffle most of our remedial devices and penal methods and who may in fact be to some degree more deeply socialized with a criminal way of life directly as a result of their experiences in Borstals and prisons. They are an altogether different group from the handful of criminals from choice, men who have made crime a more or less profitable way of life. The fortunate thing is that, at the moment, as far as we can see, in this country few juvenile offenders, other than the psychiatrically disturbed, have or are likely to have much contact with most kinds of adult offenders. While this remains so it is perhaps true to say that crime and delinquency, while continuing to grow, will remain within manageable proportions; and, at the same time, that there is also some hope that our remedial and penal services will find new and more effective ways of coping with hard-core offenders no less than with the phasic delinquencies of deprived children and youths.

# The aims of the penal system 6

Until comparatively modern times it is clear that the aims of any penal system were simply to punish malefactors and to destroy or disable individuals who opposed the power of the sovereign or the state. There was no question of doing good to those who had offended against their lords and masters or, in modern terminology, of promoting their rehabilitation. Punishments were, moreover, quick and harsh and usually little public or private pity was wasted upon those who broke the law and flouted legitimated authority.

Nowadays, however, we are more uncertain of our aims and objectives and somewhat ambivalent about the whole penological process. There is a wide measure of disagreement and even of misunderstanding between jurists, politicians, law enforcement officers and the man in the street about what our penal methods are, in fact, supposed to be doing. Criminologists, as social scientists, and penal reformers who approach the topic from their own specialized and sensitive viewpoints produce further complications and crosscurrents of opinion.

## Punishment

The majority of people would, I suspect, be still very much in favour of retribution as a major if not indeed the most important objective of penal measures. Even those who might be expected to hold a more charitable view of offenders still urge the primacy of punishment. For example, a report by a committee of the Free Church of Scotland, presented to the Assembly in Edinburgh in May 1969, advocated a return to the death penalty for homicide.[1] Every now and again pressure groups seeking the reintroduction of judicial whipping, especially for juveniles and youths found guilty of crimes of violence, make their voices heard at party political conventions or through the mass media. The revenge motif, although often hidden behind a screen of rationalization and so-called 'common sense', looks like being ineradicable since it is based, amongst other things, on simple fear that the social and legal controls may break down, and as a result normal life become impossible. I think it is important to realize that this is not an entirely groundless or irrational fear.

The idea that sanctions prevent people from breaking rules is deeply implanted in our social philosophy as every school child knows. It will take many generations of objective evidence culled from the researches of social scientists to make much of an inroad into such deeply ingrained beliefs although, it must be admitted, public opinion has come in recent years to disapprove of the more obvious pains and torments inflicted by our forefathers on felons and miscreants. The treadmill, shackles and branding iron and similar physical devices receive no support nowadays. This is probably because such treatments now appear to go beyond what is necessary to achieve the alleged penological end. The Benthamite principle that enough pain to achieve the purpose is justified but that anything beyond that point is cruelty would very likely receive the assent of the majority of citizens.

## Humanitarianism

The history of penal reform in this country, which is, of course, of comparatively recent origin, has been closely associated with prophets of the eighteenth-century Enlightenment who stressed a rational approach to every social problem. There were also strong religious influences which coalesced with the more rational utilitarian viewpoint. Certain Quaker families were especially active in the penal field and the names of the Howards and the Frys are probably the two best known in this connection.

It is one of the ironies of history that these penal reformers produced almost as much direct pain as the more brutal methods which they worked to supersede. For one thing, they held the naive view that prison could be, and ought to be, a place where personal reform of the offender might take place. To this end they advocated long periods of solitary confinement during which time the prisoner could examine his conscience, spend hours in prayerful meditation, and emerge with a purified soul and a resolve to sin no more. As Sir Walter Moberley puts it, 'It may seem odd that anyone should have expected to reform Bill Sykes by forcing him to undergo something like a compulsory religious retreat, but so it was. This belief has not stood the test of experience.'[2]

In more modern times the Howard League for Penal Reform has emerged as a pressure group, supported by intellectuals, academics and reform-minded members of the public, which has campaigned steadily, and often successfully, for more enlightened and humane methods of treatment for all kinds and classes of offenders. Though comparatively small numerically, this quite powerful pressure group has exerted a remarkable influence out of all proportion to its size on the thinking of various Home Secretaries and members of Parliament. Its stand against flogging and the death penalty are only two of the areas where its social influence and carefully prepared documentary evidence have been of probably critical importance in swinging the judgement of the legislature to moderate and rescind older and more punitive penal practices.

It is probably true to say that the growth and spread of psychological knowledge during the course of the present century, and, in more recent years, the emergence of criminology as an academic discipline have both exerted growing pressure in the direction of a more constructive penal code. By submitting existing methods to the test of empirical research, and, further, by the general spirit of critical scepticism which social science inevitably fosters, considerable doubt has been cast upon the whole of our penal system and its associated philosophy. This has reinforced the growing doubts that many serious-minded people currently have about the whole rationale of punishment and treatment of delinquents. Such doubts have created sufficient anxiety on the moral level to produce the ambivalence which, as we have already suggested, characterizes our general attitude to the more obviously punitive elements in our penal system.

Fear of the criminal is thus made even more psychologically disturbing because of our own inner feelings of uncertainty and guilt. No topic is so likely to rouse a lively debate or so sharp a division of views in almost every sector of society than the alleged growing crime wave and what we ought to do about it. This is particularly noticeable, of course, in the U.S.A. where during the presidential election of the late nineteen-sixties the subject of public law and order became a substantial political issue to which the various candidates were each obliged to proffer their proposed solutions.

*Deterrence*

The rationale of punishment has always involved the idea of retribution (an eye for an eye and a tooth for a tooth), and it has also contained the notion that those who witness the just and condign punishment of the offender will thereby be deterred from offending in similar manner. This is what is usually implied by the magisterial phrase 'I am going to make an example of you' or by the pedagogic predilection for corporal punishment in front of the other pupils. It was also the official view of the Prison Commission at the end of the last century, whose first chairman, Du Cane, epitomized the regime in terms of 'hard fare, hard labour and a hard bed'.[3]

Deterrence has both individual and general implications. Most people would probably subscribe to the view that the punished offender is likely to be put off committing the same breach again (once bitten, twice shy) since he knows the penalty he will have to pay; and also to the view that the likelihood of being punished will deter others who might be tempted in similar directions from giving way to temptation. It is, indeed, a tenet of police philosophy that certainty of arrest and punishment would greatly reduce the rates for most kinds of crime. But since there is always the hope of getting away with it and the chance of avoiding detection (a chance in some cases which is a worthwhile risk for a criminal to take), the preventive force of punishment is greatly diminished. A higher detection rate, which is the ideal the police naturally aspire to, would, so it is argued, reduce crime still further as the odds on being found out would clearly become shorter and shorter. This is a rational viewpoint and one which should be highly acceptable to latterday utilitarians.

Yet deterrence can sometimes outdo itself, as the old adage 'as well be hanged for a sheep as a lamb' suggests. Too severe a penalty for smaller crimes can drive the desperate criminal into committing the more serious offences which carry an almost identical punishment, and so actually encourage law-breaking instead of preventing it. Moreover, excessively severe punishment involving the death penalty for theft, or transportation for life for simple larcenies, often induced nineteenth century juries to acquit offenders rather than be instrumental in inflicting such heavy sentences upon their less fortunate fellow citizens. When this happens the law is in danger of being treated with contempt, and this can clearly have serious consequences for the law itself and for society in general.

So, while exemplary punishment and retribution remain widely acceptable penal principles, other considerations can be seen to have been making headway in response to humanitarian sensitivity and to the findings of criminological research. This has been particularly noticeable in regard to the treatment of children and younger offenders for whom sympathy has plainly been growing fairly steadily during the present century. The Children Act of 1908, which established special courts for juveniles, is one outstanding example of this desire to discriminate between young and older delinquents. Another is the setting up of the Borstal training service in the same year to deal with youths in isolation from older offenders and confirmed criminals. More recently all the discussion and hard work that has gone into preparing the 1969 Children and Young Persons Act can be regarded as the logical outcome of this ever-growing concern for the young as more sinned against than sinning. So, too, is the raising of the age of criminal responsibility from eight to ten years in the 1963 Act.

## *Reform*

Most people would regard the younger delinquents as potentially redeemable if only appropriate rehabilitatory means can be found for them. While they are no doubt willing to write off the confirmed adult recidivist as an almost total social loss, there is an understandable reluctance to categorize any offenders under the age of, say, twenty-one, as being beyond reclaim. Thus, we see how the notion of reform rather than retribution has been fairly rapidly making inroads into the conventional penal system. Each generation has seemed willing to go a stage further than its predecessor in promoting reform as a major treatment goal and to extend the principle moreover to older and larger groups of offenders. In this way it is hoped that juvenile delinquents will quickly come to leave their delinquent phase behind them and become adequately adjusted to the norms of the wider community, and the older youths will be resocialized before accepting for themselves the outcast status which almost inevitably leads to a life of crime. The names of Evelyn Ruggles-Brise, who founded the Borstal system, and of Alexander Paterson, a Prison Commissioner who improved it and who did so much to humanize the prisons in the nineteen-twenties, are perhaps outstanding amongst other reform-conscious civil servants who spent much of their time and energy in the rehabilitation and treatment of younger offenders, while at the civilian level, as it were, Margery Fry carried on the reforming tradition of the great Quaker families.

It is now abundantly clear that most of the changes which have been made in the penal system in the past fifty years or so have had social reclamation as one of their main objectives. This is so even in instances where severity has been stressed as, for example, in the establishment of detention centres after the 1948 Act. The 'short sharp shock' of a three or six month sentence to a detention centre which was introduced to replace the less acceptable imposition of judicial whipping, was considered to be much more constructive an approach than the birch. So, too, in the ever-extending use of probation, and more recently still in the use of open prisons and open Borstals and the innovation of an expanding parole system, we can discern similar ameliorative influences and ideas at work. This growing concern for the offender as a person who not only has a need but also a right to be rehabilitated is in line with modern sensitivities in other social fields, and is paralleled by a deepening concern for the poor, the homeless and the friendless whose lives form so sharp a contrast to those of the majority of members of the modern affluent society and welfare state. Yet, as has already been suggested, many people still cling to notions of punishment and deterrence and it takes very little to rouse public anxiety about the alleged 'softness' of modern treatment methods. Politicians are obliged to be acutely sensitive to such popular outcries and to undertake action to allay anxiety. The apparent spate of goal-breaks in 1966, and in particular the escapes of two of the great train robbers and the spy George Blake, which led to the enquiry under the direction of Earl Mountbatten and the subsequent clamping down of fresh controls in prison in order to achieve maximum security, is a good illustration of this close interaction between press and public panic and the reactions of the authorities.

But it must also be said that public outcry and press reporting is not confined to gaol breaks or similar threats to the community. It can also occur when attention is drawn to breaches of regulations by prison officers or headmasters of approved schools. Excessive and illegal use of the cane at Court Lees Approved School, for example, after being leaked to the press by one of the teaching staff, led to an immediate enquiry and the removal of the headmaster and the deputy head, and to the closure and subsequent re-opening of the school under a new name and new managers. So, too, allegations of unnecessary use of physical force by the staff at Reading Borstal in 1968 led to a similar enquiry and the closure of the Borstal and the re-opening of the building as a prison.

The public is sensitive, it seems, to excessive leniency and almost equally to any sign of brutality in its penal institutions and child reformatories. This is probably why Home Secretaries and government in general are much more go-ahead in promoting penal reforms than popular approval would very likely support. The humanitarian pressure group and the opinions of sociological and psychological experts often get put into practice before the public as a whole is really ready for them, as the abolition of capital punishment demonstrates. At the same time the ambivalence prevails and breaks surface every now and again, as when, following the Court Lees scandal, the Home Secretary promised that the use of the cane would be phased out in approved schools. But later reports, however, have indicated that in the future, at the community homes the new Children Act is to set up, its use will still not be officially banned.

There is therefore a kind of running counterpoint in penal practice between the reformatory humanitarian theme and the retributionist punitive theme, the one or the other becoming dominant as it is evoked by some new event, such as a gaol-break or a research report, and the public's reaction, sparked off and fed by the journalists and broadcasters' comments.

At the time of writing, however (1974), it appears that reform is—temporarily at least—in the ascendancy, as is evidenced by the development of new, non-residential treatments for both juvenile and adult offenders. Intermediate treatment programmes for adolescents, community service orders for both adults and juveniles, and day training centres as alternatives to prison for the over-twenty-ones, witness to a growing awareness of the need to rehabilitate offenders and to reconcile them to the community they have transgressed against.

Subsidiary aims in penology worthy of a brief mention are restitution and compensation. Simple human justice seems to require that an injured party should be compensated for his loss or injury, preferably by the person or persons responsible for it. Stolen goods should be returned to their owners, victims of assault or rape should be compensated financially. This is good both for the victim and for the offender who is obliged to make up for the trouble and injury he had caused. Margery Fry campaigned for many years that the interests of the victim should not get overlooked by our concern for the punishment or rehabilitation of the offender. One result of her campaign has been the institution by government of a limited scheme whereby the victims of certain kinds of offence may receive compensation out of public funds.* But the principle of restitution

* More than £1 million was paid out to victims of violence in 1967 to 3,490 individual claimants. By 1972 the total had risen to 9,886 and the amount paid out reached £3.28 million.

by the offender is much more complex than simple notions of justice might suggest. Usually the offender has simply not got the financial means to repay the harm he has done and, in the case of children who have done extensive damage, the idea that their parents could be expected to pay out several thousand pounds by way of damages is clearly an impossibility.

*Social defence*
An overall consideration in any penal system must involve as a constant and abiding principle the safeguarding of public order and the protection of the community in general. This idea has received a growing amount of attention in recent years, especially at criminological conferences and similar gatherings, under the somewhat modish concept of 'social defence'. This has a strong utilitarian flavour and hence is very appealing to those rationalists who seek to rid the penal system of any trace of personal taint or public malice. It implies a large-scale endeavour to prevent criminogenic situations developing and the building into the life and institutions of society services which, in the medical sphere, would be classified as good sanitation. Traditional ideas of justice do, however, seem likely to cut across any large scale attempt to deal with offenders *before* they have committed their offence. The Queen of Hearts' cry of 'off with his head!' has some kind of logic behind it if we could only be sure that we could always pick out the future villain and never select an innocent by mistake. The concept of preventive detention set up after the 1948 Act but now somewhat discredited was clearly based on the social defence notion, but only for those who already had a long record of crime behind them and had been apprehended again for similar offences. It has also been more or less accepted, too, for some juveniles brought before the courts as being in need of care or protection or in moral danger or beyond control. But in these cases it is the future welfare of the individual child rather than the protection of the community that is the primary purpose of such an exercise.

There would obviously be a danger if social defence principles were to be adopted merely for the convenience of the police. The loitering with felonious intent charge which can be made at the moment or a similar and rather more substantive charge of being in possession of 'house-breaking implements' are no doubt helpful in checking likely offences, but they could also be used to persecute undesirables and vagrants or as a means of tormenting incorrigibles and old lags.

It is not easy, therefore, to see social defence principles making very much headway in a society composed of individuals who are hypersensitive to threats to their freedom of action. Fascist and totalitarian states, of course, have frequent recourse to it for their own dubious and undemocratic ends. Even in the field of juvenile delinquency, where prevention of further deterioration is, perhaps, a genuinely-held objective on the part of the authorities, it is clear that some criminologists see serious dangers to individual freedom existing. Arguments against the treatment of juvenile offenders outside the court are often supported by the fear that less than justice may be done even where provision is made for the child who denies his guilt. There is also at the time of writing a debate in progress, which journalistically has been interpreted as 'depraved or deprived', which centres around the provision of community homes for children who have broken the law or committed acts which as adults would have brought them into a court, where they would live together with children who have not broken the law. The issue is a genuine one, however bedevilled by partisan viewpoints and special pleading. The fact that at present we send both delinquents and non-delinquents to community homes should not affect judgement as to the wisdom or desirability of such a policy. Do delinquents contaminate non-delinquents? Are children who steal really to be thought of as deprived? If so, why does one deprived child steal and another merely run away from home or truant from school?

Answers to these questions are not yet available as a result of scientific research. Until they are, it would seem a sensible policy to treat thieves differently from those in moral danger or abandoned by their parents. Perhaps the truth is that delinquency is at its root a symptom of some kind of deprivation within the home or social environment or both. Perhaps the appropriate way to deal with all deprived children is to put them in new environments where their specific deficiencies can be compensated for—if that is humanly possible. Again we do not know what the truth is. Again we must wait for fundamental social research to enlighten us. But the fact is that the philosophy underpinning the 1969 Children and Young Persons Act *assumes* that the answers to such questions are already known, and as a community we are busily proceeding along the assumption that there is no fundamental difference between the delinquent child and the disturbed and endangered child. Would such a philosophy, one wonders, in time come to be logically extended to include the adult offenders? And if so what would the consequences be for notions of culpability and autonomy and for penology generally?

A modern approach which seeks to make use of predictive devices to crime which we shall be discussing in more detail later raises the same moral problems. The Gluecks in America and Dr D. H. Stott in this country have strenuously advocated the application of predictive techniques to the child population to try to sort out the possible sheep from the potential goats so that, as far as the latter are concerned, preventive and remedial work can be undertaken with them at a time when it might have the best prospect of success. But here again mistakes can so easily be made and no predictive method is likely to be right in, at most, more than three-quarters of cases. And are there not grave risks of individuals being stigmatized as delinquency-prone? We know how children with low I.Qs. have been identified and written off as academic failures. This is a serious enough stigma for anyone to have to overcome but would not the label of delinquency-prone be even more damaging and in the event self-fulfilling?

So the arguments go on and there is little or no certainty for any group of legislators to found a secure penal system upon. Fashion also plays a part in throwing up new ideas for treatment and disposal, and there is often in the criminological and social-work fields, as in other walks of life, the notorious band-wagon mentality and halo-effect of a new idea or a fresh minted theory.

*Crime as a social process*
In concluding this section it might perhaps be worth noting that in a

very real sense criminals are products of a social process of which the law and its allied penal system are constituent parts. One of the errors which criminological research in the past tended to commit arose because, as Leslie Wilkins has well said, 'a disproportionate amount of attention has been given to the consideration of the offender as an individual and too little to the system with which his behaviour represents an interaction'.[4] This resulted in excessive absorption with the psychological or the psychiatric state of the offender and almost no concern for the ways whereby 'the law and its instrumentalities help to produce the defiant, anti-social state of mind basic to the criminal role'.[5]

The key concept which connects the psychological with the sociological understanding of behaviour is the self-image. As we have argued earlier, if an individual comes to accept a self-image which is anti-social, delinquent and deviant, then his social rehabilitation becomes accordingly the harder to effect. But it is as much the result of his involvement in a social process as his own psychological condition that produces the end product: there is, in fact, a continual interaction between individual personality and social experience, and in this dynamic interplay it is unnecessary in most instances to attempt to assign priority or supremacy to either the psychic or the social process.

The fundamental problem that faces even the most enlightened penal system is how to change the offender's self-image after he has become the object of trial and incarceration without giving the impression that the law is unimportant. At the earlier, juvenile stage it boils down to how to reassure the child that he is an object of love and concern without the abandonment of discipline. As Croft and Grygier showed in their very interesting sociometric study of schoolboys, some of whom were truants and delinquents, in most classes the latter were rejected by conformists, and those who were rated badly by their teachers were also the least popular with the other boys.[6] In this small study we can see how powerful sections of the wider society also tend to reject and isolate deviants and so confirm them in the role they have partly helped to create for themselves but which also has partly been thrust upon them. Croft and Grygier showed, too, that, in the backward classes in the school, boys who were 'well-behaved' were not especially popular nor were those who 'behaved badly' automatically rejected.

Aaron Cicourel has also argued in a much longer and more complex study that the delinquent may be seen as an emergent social product, transformed over a period of time by a sequence of encounters with police, magistrates and probation officers into a social deviant.[7] From this kind of analysis we can understand how problematic the nature of social control and juridical procedures are, and how in their own way they contribute to the total crime problem.

Stanley Cohen's study of the 'Mods and Rockers' phenomenon in the mid-nineteen-sixties shows how easily public anxiety can be whipped up to a state of near-hysteria by excessive publicity in the media, and how comparatively mild examples of teenage boisterousness can be interpreted as serious threats to law and order by over-reactive observers and by magistrates in particular.[8]

It would be naive, however, to infer from the evidence of Cicourel or Croft and Grygier that, because taking action against offenders may in certain instances be a contributory factor in their further delinquency, the community ought to do nothing about them. We are here up against the basic dilemma which faces every society which is obliged for obvious reasons to impose some regulations on the behaviour of its citizens yet which from considerations of humanity and morality does not wish to alienate individuals or to outlaw non-conforming groups. It is precisely because many people are conscious of this dilemma that a generally ambivalent attitude towards the enforcement of the law, to the police and the prison officers whose job it is to enforce it can be found. If only punishment did reform the delinquent our minds would be a lot easier. But unfortunately we now know that punishment can often have the exactly opposite effect. So our uncertainty grows and we turn rather desperately to the invention of more and more new methods and procedures in the hope that they will provide viable solutions to our penological and moral problems. At the same time, as we have already seen, crime rates over a long period of time tend to rise fairly steadily in spite of changes in administration, new methods of social intervention and fresh forms of treatment.* This, as we have already hinted, may be partly due to the fact that we are expending our energies unprofitably and failing to come to grips with the profound sociological forces which contribute to crime and delinquency as elements in ongoing social processes which are far from being merely abnormal or pathological in our culture.

---

* The prison population is, however, now falling, having dropped from some 40,000 in 1971 to only 38,000 in 1972, probably because of changes in sentencing practice rather than of a fall in the amount of serious crime.

# The treatment of offenders 7

As we have already seen, a crucial distinction has come to be made in our attitudes towards juvenile and adult offenders and accordingly their methods of treatment and disposal are noticeably different. Generally speaking, the treatment of young offenders is intended to be less punitive and more reformatory, although there are, of course, exceptions to this generalization, notably in the establishment of detention centres with their deliberately repressive regime.

*Disposal of juveniles*

The setting up of special courts to deal with juveniles (at the moment over ten† and under seventeen years of age) is paralleled by the provision of specialized institutions in which children and young people are segregated from adults and submitted to a course of disciplined re-education. Remedial measures which, at the time of writing, are provided for juveniles consist of a wide range of options some of which, such as fining, are largely admonitory while others, such as committal to community homes* or to a Borstal, are intended to deal with fairly deep-seated delinquent attitudes and proclivities. All such measures have in recent years come in for a great deal of public discussion and all have been or are in course of being reshaped by the new Children and Young Persons Act of 1969.

Since radical changes are now on foot it is not necessary to give here more than a brief summary of the established methods for treating young offenders. These may be divided into penal and non-penal procedures. Penal treatment can only follow a finding of guilt in a juvenile court where the proceedings are laid down by rules which

† In practice, however, only children who commit 'serious' offences who are under twelve years of age are taken to court.

* Until recently called approved schools and known earlier as reformatories.

have the force of statutory law. They involve, amongst other things, the taking of formal evidence, the exclusion of the public, a limitation upon press reporting so that a child cannot be mentioned by name, and where possible the attendance of parents in order to give the child support, and reports by social workers and teachers to fill in for the magistrates relevant background information and details of a child's life history. Juvenile courts are obliged by their terms of reference to have regard to the welfare of the child as well as the protection of society. This sometimes involves a dilemma which different benches resolve in different ways. Generally speaking, however, since most childish offences do not involve socially serious issues and grave charges such as rape or armed robbery, the dichotomy between the welfare and the penal aspects of the court's functions does not present many problems. In run-of-the-mill cases the prevention of a child's further descent into criminality is clearly seen as the principal concern of the bench, although it must be admitted that some magistrates stress punishment rather than rehabilitation when coming to their decisions.

The court has a variety of treatment methods to apply to children found guilty of offences which roughly can be ranked in terms of gravity as follows:

1. *Discharge*. This can be either conditional or absolute. The former is a very frequent method of disposal for minor and first offenders and may usually be interpreted as a severe kind of warning not to offend again.

2. *Fines*. There are statutory limitations controlling the amount of fine which can be imposed on juveniles; these are always paid by parents in the case of offenders under fourteen and even in the case of older children courts can order the parents to pay. Some courts make very frequent use of fining as it is clearly punitive and prevents an offender or his family thinking that he has got away scot free with his delinquency.

3. *Attendance Centre*. Attendance centres were set up by the 1948 Criminal Justice Act so that magistrates could inflict a mild form of punishment upon children who are being a nuisance and seem to be

in need of a check. Centres operate on Saturday afternoons and are usually staffed by police officers. Their programme includes drill, handicrafts, instruction in first aid and similar useful leisure-time activities, all carried out under rather strict conditions. While the curtailment of a boy's weekend leisure is perceived as punitive, a genuine attempt is made to occupy the time (usually twelve hours spread over six consecutive Saturdays) during which attendance is compulsory in constructive ways which could conceivably help in character building were they to be followed for a longer period. A Cambridge study of the work of attendance centres carried out by McClintock in the early nineteen-sixties indicated that they have most success when dealing with offenders who have little or no previous delinquency history, but are much less successful with those who are more habituated and who have already had experience of other forms of treatment.[4] As a form of disposal it may well be that attendance centres in the future will become merged into various other more constructive and community-based programmes.

4. *Probation.* Probation is at present in a state of change and transition. While it is intended at some future date that the supervision of the under-seventeens will be entirely the responsibility of social workers in the new personal service departments set up following the Seebohm Committee report, at the present time magistrates can and do ask probation officers to supervise children from the age of fourteen onwards, and the local authority social workers and probation officers in some areas decide to share the supervisory task together. In addition, of course, the probation service has had its duties greatly increased by the extension of after-care responsibilities for those discharged from detention centres, Borstals and prisons, and has in fact recently been re-named the Probation and After-Care Department.

A probation order involved a child or young person being placed under the direct supervision of one of the court's probation officers for periods of one, two or three years as might be deemed most suitable. The probation service, which grew historically out of the police court missionaries of Victorian days, was set up by the 1907

Act and has never been thought of as specifically for juveniles. From its inception its purpose has been rehabilitative and its methods based upon the strength of personal relationship and the building up of reciprocal respect between officer and client. In more recent years probation officers have come to think of themselves as professional caseworkers and the majority receive training of varying lengths either on Home Office courses or at courses run in connection with university extra-mural and social science departments. Probation officers are regarded as experts in the field of delinquency, some specialized in working with children. As committed social workers, most seem to have a truly missionary or reformist outlook and to have a high degree of identification with offenders and interest in their welfare which goes beyond the performance of a routine job. This welfare outlook can sometimes conflict with their responsibility to the courts as when, for example, one of their probationers breaks the law while under supervision. In such cases it is probably the officer's duty to bring the probationer before the court again but, on balance, he may consider such a step psychologically dangerous in certain cases and a genuine dilemma can occur.

The success of probation is particularly difficult to study since the probationer remains at large throughout the treatment process and is hence constantly subjected to a wide range of environmental influences other than the casework relationship with the officer. Moreover, as in all social and penal work, problems of criteria for success and failure are open to dispute. By taking a comparatively crude and simple yardstick of whether or not the probationer was brought back to court again either for a breach of the order or for a further offence during the period of supervision, members of the Cambridge Department of Criminal Science,* in their study of 28,000 persons placed on probation in 1956, discovered that 79 per cent of the adults and 73 per cent of the juveniles successfully completed their probation. This group was then followed up for a three-year period and it was found that, when judged by these more exacting criteria, 70 per cent of the adults and only 57 per cent of the

* Now the Cambridge Institute of Criminology.

juveniles still retained unblemished records. Females were more successful probationers than males, and those with a previous period of institutional treatment were more likely to revert to crime than those who had never been in an approved school, Borstal or prison.[2]

The fact that children on the whole seem to do less well on probation than adults suggests that casework relationships are more meaningful when applied to adults because adults conceivably have more understanding and concern about their socially dangerous condition and hence may be more inclined to co-operate with the probation officers. In recent years some probation officers, dissatisfied with their traditional one-to-one relationship with their teenage clients, have experimented with small groups, making use of discussion or activities or a combination of both. Only a very small minority have undertaken such group work with juvenile probationers and the usefulness of such methods has not been objectively evaluated, but it represents a tendency which is likely to become more important in the future when probation work becomes more closely associated with other ameliorative projects and agencies on a wider community-based foundation.

An ingenious research project which Leslie Wilkins devised and carried out in the nineteen-fifties, in which he endeavoured to compare the comparative effectiveness of probation and other methods of disposal, failed to show that probation was likely to be any more effective than other methods when applied indiscriminately.[3] Part of the skill in sentencing clearly involves being able to distinguish the good from the bad risks and, as far as probation goes, first offenders are not so likely to have such low reconviction rates as they might under some other measures, for example, fining. At the same time, it must be emphasized that, by its very nature, probation always entails some degree of risk which cannot be eliminated however careful we are.

A more sensitive and effective sentencing policy will only come as the result of long-term and subtle research. The Home Office Research Unit has been engaged on such a study for a number of years and some useful information has already been published in connection with its enquiry into the effects of probation. Martin

Davies's report, based on a study of the social environment of a group of males aged seventeen to twenty, revealed that 37·3 per cent of the group were reconvicted within a year of the order being made.[4] He uncovered factors which seemed to be closely associated with reconviction, such as the probationer's relationship with his father, whether he was employed or not at the time when the order was made, and the influence of the peer group—all of which seem to be in harmony with sociological theory about the nature of juvenile crime. Factors such as the influence of the mother, the presence or not of a girl-friend, and the degree of overcrowding in the home, were adjudged to have no significant association with the reconviction of probationers. Research reports such as this one by Davies should in time give assistance to magistrates and social workers in deciding which children should be put on supervision orders and which ones are much greater risks. As the local authority social service departments take over supervision of juveniles it is to be hoped that they will make use of these and similar research findings as well as be prepared to draw on the long experience of probation officers in carrying on such work.

5. *Supervision.* Since the passing of the Children and Young Persons Act of 1969 courts now make supervision in place of probation orders for all children under seventeen who are found to be delinquent. This follows naturally on from the former practice of making Fit Person orders for either the deprived or neglected children as initiated by earlier Child Care legislation. In effect what is now happening is that local authority Child Care departments are absorbed into a generic social service which is designed to provide a comprehensive service for all children who in any way are deemed to be in need of care, protection or control. In the case of children found guilty of a criminal offence they can be handed over to the local authority social workers in similar manner and their ultimate disposal and treatment will be decided by them and no longer by the magistrates.

6. *Community Home (formerly Approved School).* As their name implies, these schools or homes are not managed by the Prison

Department of the Home Office. Some are set up by local authorities but the majority are still run by voluntary bodies including the Churches. Their regimes are, however, subject to state control by regulations made by the Home Secretary and through official inspection. They are nowadays all residential and are, of course, the modern counterparts of the old Victorian reformatories and industrial schools. A rudimentary classificatory system operates so that children committed to them do receive the benefit of a regime which is supposed to meet their individual needs. Boys are, of course, segregated from girls, younger children from older children and Catholics from non-Catholics, and some of the institutions attempt to specialize in the treatment of children of high or low I.Q. Almost all are 'open' institutions, in so far as they are not fenced in, and absconding is fairly common. Special high-security units are provided within existing establishments for chronic absconders and similar cases of high risk or danger.

Children can be committed to a community home or to an approved school because they have been found guilty of the kind of offence which in the case of an adult would have resulted in imprisonment but they can also be sent there if they are adjudged to be in need of care or protection or if they are deemed to be beyond parental control, or truanting, or if they are not responding to a supervision order. Commitment is for varying periods but may be three years or even longer in the case of children who have not yet completed their formal educational requirements up to the fifteenth year. The school managers can send a child back home after six months' schooling provided they think it desirable on general grounds, but after-care requirements operate for them as for those staying on longer for at least two and sometimes even three years. The after-care is nowadays being carried out by local authority social workers in the area where the child's home is located.

Community homes are often defended on the grounds that they are primarily concerned with training and education and not institutions designed to punish young offenders. A great amount of time is spent in actual learning and in sports and pastimes which in other contexts would be considered both normal and pleasurable.

At the same time, the children themselves probably perceive them as mainly punitive and retaliatory, and certainly there was some evidence that some magistrates used to speak of them and regard them as ultimate sanctions for those who will not mend their ways and respond to non-residential and presumably 'milder' methods of treatment. Furthermore, every now and again the public became aware of irregularities within schools and of punishment being inflicted on inmates which exceeded not only what may be reasonable but which were also, more seriously, actual breaches of the law. It is this latter aspect which was particularly distressing. While there are many authenticated accounts of brutality at private schools which are deemed to be catering for 'normal' children, it is especially disturbing that children who had been sent at the behest of the courts to residential schools which were in theory concerned with their readjustment to the social norms should themselves, as part of that training process, have been exposed to illegal practices. The Court Lees scandal to which reference has earlier been made, was clearly no isolated phenomenon. We had the Carlton school affair some years earlier and shortly after we had the removal of the head of an approved school in the Isle of Wight, run by the De La Salle Brothers, for having punished boys 'with excessive severity'.

Such evidence as that cited above, and it cannot be lightly dismissed, indicates very clearly what I have referred to in the previous chapter as our general ambivalence with regard to the treatment of those who break the law, and highlights once again the dichotomous themes of retribution and reform, rejection and rehabilitation, which plague our penal and reformatory system. A great deal of dissatisfaction has collected around the approved school regime in recent years and at times their staffs appear to be very much on the defensive. The reformatory work of such educational experimenters as David Wills,[5] George Lyward,[6] Otto Shaw,[7] and F. G. Llenhoff[8] is very much an active criticism of the methods used in more conventional schools for disturbed and maladjusted children (many of whom are, of course, also delinquent) and there is little doubt that the pressure of informed opinion has veered towards a more relaxed atmosphere and individuated treatment for those unfortunate children whose social deprivation and emotional maldevelopment brings them into early conflict with the laws of society. The concept of community homes which have now superseded the earlier approved schools, while many still have to fight against stubborn opposition from some of the older members of approved school and remand home staff, shows that the pioneering work of Homer Lane and his modern successors has become the new orthodoxy.[9]

The transition from approved school to community home cannot be magically effected merely by changing the name. As Owen Gill has shown in his study of a school in transition, there are many obstacles in the institutions themselves and in the ingrained views of children committed to them which make it difficult to substitute the more modern notion of individual treatment for the older concept of training within a disciplined group setting.[10]

But the ultimate test which will be applied to whatever institutions are devised to cope with young offenders will surely be whether or not they reduce the rates of re-conviction and promote children's readjustment to normal social life. And on this score it is admitted that approved school success rates have been falling in recent years. A revised Home Office formula of assessment which included only those found guilty of indictable and of the more serious of non-indictable offences during a two-year follow-up period showed, for example, that, for the year 1962, 55 per cent of boys and 17 per cent of girls released from approved schools were reconvicted.[11]

Reasons for the high and probably growing failure rates for ex-approved school inmates are partly to be found in the nature of the regimes themselves, partly, without doubt, in the changes that have come upon society in general. Not only are correctional institutions operating against a widespread atmosphere of ever-increasing permissiveness and tolerance for deviations, but there is a growing feeling amongst significant sections of youth that many of the existing values and standards are hypocritical and outmoded. In a social climate characterized by so much doubt, ambivalence, contradiction and flux it is really not very surprising that unstable children and emotionally disturbed young people react more quickly than others, with the result that law enforcement at all levels and in relation to both treatment and prevention becomes increasingly more complex and difficult:

7. *Detention Centre.* Detention centres, which were established by the 1948 Act, are to be thought of as alternatives to prison for young males and also to some extent as substitutes for judicial corporal punishment which was abolished at the same time. They are divided at the age of fourteen into junior and senior institutions and unlike the approved schools have no intermediate grade. They are intended to deal with tough youngsters, administering 'a short, sharp reminder' that their delinquent behaviour is no longer to be tolerated. Their regime was originally harsh and still is highly disciplinary. The smallest offence, for example an undone button on parade, tends to be met with instant punishment in the form of extra work and fatigues, while more serious internal offences result in the loss of remission of sentence. They are perhaps the nearest civil institution we have in this country to the military 'glasshouse'.

The usual period of sentence is for three months but a maximum of six months is permitted. In their early days it is clear that many unsuitable youngsters were sent to detention centres, youths suffering from psychiatric afflictions for whom the regime was never intended, but in recent years greater discrimination has been practised. In spite of the fact that detention centres have been unfavourably commented upon by criminologists, magistrates and Home Office spokesmen seem to be pleased with their availability and their numbers have been steadily increased since their inception. By 1969 there were in operation fourteen senior and five junior centres for boys and one for girls.*

Elizabeth Field has brought together the findings of the relevant research which has so far been done on the work of the detention centres.[12] Certain broad conclusions emerge. The most common offences for which detention orders are made for boys involve offences against property, taking and driving away a motor vehicle, and violence; while for the girls breaches of probation orders come second to offences against property, followed by sexual misdemeanours.

* This has now been closed.

Reconviction rates for most of the offenders studied so far are fairly similar for all groups over a two year follow-up period and are between thirty-six and fifty-five per cent. Most researchers agree that the first six months after release is crucial and that this is the time when relapse into delinquency is most likely to occur. After care for ex-detainees was not applied in the early years of youth detention, no doubt because the severity of the discipline imposed and the social

TABLE 2
*Detention Centres   1967 figures*

| Year | Years at risk | Number discharged | Not reconvicted % | Reconvicted % |
| --- | --- | --- | --- | --- |
| *Senior Centres* | | | | |
| 1964 | 3 | 3984 | 41·9 | 58·1 |
| 1965 | 2 | 5144 | 49·7 | 50·3 |
| 1966 | 1 | 5712 | 66·4 | 33·6 |
| *Junior Centres* | | | | |
| 1964 | 3 | 1278 | 36·5 | 63·5 |
| 1965 | 2 | 1236 | 45·1 | 54·9 |
| 1966 | 1 | 1310 | 61·8 | 38·2 |

Source. *Report on the work of the Prison Department 1967*, Statistical Tables.

distance which divided officers from boys made the usefulness of such a service highly problematic. In recent years, however, compulsory supervision has been imposed for a period of twelve months with the sanction of recall for two weeks' further incarceration should the discharged young person's conduct prove unsatisfactory. Recall has in fact seldom been used, probably because of the disruption it might cause to the programmes of existing centres.

As far as can be seen at the present time, detention centres may possibly be phased out of existence in the not too distant future as may also be the fate of Borstals and young prisoners' centres, and a new type of as yet unnamed residential institution may be created to take their place. The idea of a parole system for young offenders is also under discussion and could come into being during the late nineteen-seventies.

8. *Borstal*. Borstals were from their earliest foundation concerned with training and re-education rather than with punishment although, like detention centres, they are run and administered by the Prison Department of the Home Office. Borstals are mainly for boys between the ages of fifteen and twenty-one but two or three are maintained for girls who are deemed intractable to non-institutional treatment. Only higher courts can order a young person to be committed to a Borstal\* although juvenile courts are allowed to forward a recommendation to that effect in the case of older youths who are thought to require training away from their home environment. The courts do not determine the length of residence which may in the event be as short as six months or as long as two years. The tendency nowadays is to discharge wherever possible shortly after a twelve-month stay, the average being round about fourteen months. The decision to release is made by the staff of the institution in consultation with the official visitors and with the final approval of the Prison Department. A long-standing after-care system is in operation which covers two years from the date of discharge.

Borstals, like approved schools, have classificatory systems and there are both 'open' and 'closed' types of institutions. Gaynes Hall caters for boys with high I.Qs. while Feltham specializes in psychiatric cases, and several have been experimenting in recent years with group discussions between staff and inmates and with casework approaches. There are now over 5,500 young people in Borstals at the present time and this greatly enlarged inmate population, plus the fact that some of the more amenable youngsters are nowadays sent to detention centres instead of to Borstals, has contributed to a lowering of morale in the service due to falling success rates. Furthermore, changed social conditions and new attitudes have made the original regime, which was firmly based on the more spartan aspects

---

\* Except in the case of absconders from approved schools or 'trouble makers' in approved schools whom magistrates can commit directly to a Borstal.

of the British public school model, less suited to the new generation of inmates. That all is not well with the system can be seen, for example, by complaints made in the press in 1968 about conditions in the allocation centre at Wormwood Scrubs Prison when it became clear that boys were kept far too long waiting for allocation in conditions described as 'filthy, insanitary and disgusting' by visiting magistrates; by the complaints made about physical violence at Reading already referred to; and by the admitted high failure rates that are now becoming common.[13] T. C. N. Gibbens found that the failure rate for the group of 198 Borstal boys studied during the early nineteen-fifties was as high as 53 per cent after five years discharge.[14] Dr Hood made a valuable study of two groups of homeless boys discharged from Borstals in 1953 and 1957 respectively, one of which was discharged before the new after-care arrangements were available in the mid-nineteen-fifties, and the other of which received the benefit of the new programme. During a two-year follow-up he found that those boys who had enjoyed the new after-care help did no better than those who had not received it. The highest failure rate was amongst boys who had a previous history of institutionalization of four and a half years or more irrespective of the quality of after care they had received. No less than three-quarters were reconvicted at least twice after discharge.[15]

Dr Hood's study is disturbing for three reasons. First, because it showed that improved after care did not produce better results; second, because it suggests a worsening response to supervision generally; and third, because it challenges the value of institutionalized treatment for the more 'passive inadequate delinquents' who seem to comprise the homeless Borstal failure group and who, presumably, grow up into the habitual inmates of adult prisons.

It would be wrong, however, to give the impression that existing Borstals are failing all along the line. Dr Cockett[16] has found that they somewhat surprisingly do best with the least promising material, and Gibbens came to much the same conclusion in his study earlier referred to in this chapter. Gibbens *et al.* found that the greatest Borstal risks were likely to be youths judged to be psychiatrically normal but who had 'anti-social associations' from an early age.

Conversely, they found that 'the nearer the abnormality to mental illness, the better the criminal prognosis', a finding that suggests that greater care in allocation and the provision of more extensive psychological examination and help might materially improve Borstal success rates in the future.

TABLE 3
*Borstal Reconvictions    1967 figures*

|  | Year | Years outside | Number discharged | Not reconv % | Reconvicted % Not recomm | Recommitted |
|---|---|---|---|---|---|---|
| *Boys* | | | | | | |
| | 1964 | 3 | 3429 | 29·5 | 20·3 | 52·4 |
| | 1965 | 2 | 3004 | 38·3 | 18·9 | 42·8 |
| | 1966 | 1 | 4358 | 58·7 | 14·1 | 27·2 |
| *Girls* | | | | | | |
| | 1964 | 3 | 142 | 56·3 | 16·2 | 27·5 |
| | 1965 | 2 | 131 | 63·4 | 20·6 | 16·0 |
| | 1966 | 1 | 125 | 77·6 | 10·4 | 12·0 |

Two Borstal institutions, one at Hindley in Lancashire and the other at Hewell Grange in Worcestershire, have recently been designated as neighbourhood Borstals to serve inmates coming from their surrounding localities. This experiment is designed to make interaction between home and institution easier and more meaningful, and also to permit local probation officers to maintain contact with young offenders throughout their period in Borstal.

9. *Prison.* Imprisonment of young offenders has been drastically reduced in recent years. The present position is that no court is permitted to send a juvenile to prison, although in exceptional cases of very serious crime such as homicide, juveniles may be detained during Her Majesty's pleasure in approved schools, Borstals and institutions for the mentally abnormal, and also in special young prisoners' wings of main prisons. Young adults over seventeen but under twenty-one are not eligible for approved schools but they can still be sent to Borstals or, if they require only a short period of

training, to detention centres. Those who are judged to need three years are committed to prison, but strenuous attempts are being made to prevent all but the most hardened young people from receiving prison sentences. This is very much in keeping with informed public opinion which deplores the possibility of contamination by older criminals which prison sentences may involve. When committed to prison, of course, those under twenty-one are placed in special wings but otherwise their regime is not very different from that undergone by mature offenders.

While we have touched on all the main ways of treating delinquent children and young people, one or two other methods of disposal should be mentioned before passing on to consider the provision for adults or to discuss the ethos and rationale of future developments in the child care field. Probation can be ordered in conjunction with a condition that the child will reside at an approved address or with relatives or in a probation hostel or other approved home. This step is usually taken when it is considered to be desirable to break a young person's associations in his home neighbourhood, and residents at probation hostels like those in approved lodgings or living with relatives are free to go out to their daily work like other youths. Not many youngsters are dealt with in this way, although there is a fairly strong body of opinion which favours the provision of more such hostels on the grounds that life there would be controlled but would remain near enough to ordinary home conditions to be tolerable. Moreover, they would be much cheaper to run than approved schools since inmates' earnings would help to some extent to reduce costs.

Detention in remand homes at one time was resorted to for punitive purposes in addition to using such institutions as places of safety. Punitive detention has, however, now been eliminated. The normal use of remand homes to provide a place of safety or security for children in trouble, or as 'observation centres' where young offenders can be studied by various social and psychological experts before a final decision is made regarding their future, remains.

*Disposal of adults*

Generally speaking, methods of dealing with convicted adults are less flexible and more openly punitive than methods of dealing with young delinquents. While similar procedures exist for coping with the less serious offences in the way of cautioning, fining, and discharge, the only common practice which spans all age ranges is, of course, probation. Probation, as we have already seen, is especially suitable for adults since it does not lessen their earning power or seriously limit their freedom of movement, while at the same time it makes professional advice and supervision available. Adults, moreover, are known to be more responsive than juveniles to this form of treatment, and there seems little doubt that its use could be still further extended and so help to reduce the overcrowding of the prison population. Nevertheless, courts seem to evidence a peculiar reluctance to extend the use of probation and, as far as magistrates' courts go, there has been an actual decrease in probation orders for adult offenders in the post-war years as compared to the nineteen-thirties. All too often courts resort to fining which is quicker, cheaper and more obviously punitive, and the probability that an offender will be fined has shown a remarkable rise in recent years. It is possible that this is to some extent attributable to fuller employment and greater individual financial means, but it may also have some connection with the ever increasing volume of offenders that have to be dealt with. It is also conceivable that both magistrates and the public still retain a sneaking idea that probation is really a kind of let-off, especially perhaps in the case of adults. However, with the new legislation which will make the child care rather than the probation service responsible for the under-seventeen age group, and with the growing burden of prison after-care and parole placed on the shoulders of probation officers, it is possible that magistrates and judges will come in time to see probation as a primarily adult treatment, and as a result make much more use of it than has been the case up to now.

*Prisons*

Imprisonment for non-political malefactors is, historically speaking, a comparatively modern device. Most prison sentences are of very short duration, and the great majority are detained in gaol for between three to six months. In so short a time nothing remotely resembling treatment can possibly be expected nor is it attempted. Their purpose was and still probably is mainly retributive and punitive. The local prisons to which short stay prisoners go seem designed to dismay visitors and dragoon inmates into conformity with a dreary routinized system which involves long periods of idleness locked up in unpleasant and often smelly cells, with minimal recreational facilities and overcrowding to such an extent that contamination and sexual malpractices seem to be positively encouraged. It is, moreover, still possible to be sent to prison for debt in this country. In 1966 over three thousand debtors were imprisoned, and so far we have not been able to think of any more constructive and less expensive and less degrading way of compelling people to meet their financial commitments. The sanction of attaching debtors' future earnings, although in practice in a limited way since the late nineteen-fifties, has not been very effective since those so treated frequently change their jobs and place of residence and thus are able to shake off legal pursuit. A man who is determined to avoid his debts can usually do so provided he is prepared to pay the price of a nomadic existence and is not concerned about social status and social success.

Local prisons such as Walton and Pentonville receive many different categories of prisoners, including those on remand (many of whom are ultimately found not guilty) and, when the death penalty was in operation, condemned murderers. Regional and central prisons are intended for special, usually long-term inmates, such as those serving sentences of preventive detention or correction, as those regimes were called before the Criminal Justice Bill 1966. Corrective training, which was designed to treat younger persistent offenders in the hope of their social redemption before a whole life would be spent in crime, was never very widely used and was falling into disuse even before the new Act. Preventive detention, which was designed to safeguard society from the depredations of recidivists and chronic repeaters, is still practised although no longer under that name, and persistent offenders can be held for up to ten years under extended sentence orders. Criminologists are almost unanimously averse to preventive detention and to extended sentences and the courts, too, seem to be inclined to make decreasing use of disposal methods which are purely custodial, especially as the majority of such offenders are not by any stretch of the imagination to be thought of as serious threats to the community.

There are two important facts about imprisonment in this country. First, the prison population continues to grow steadily.* In 1968, for instance, the daily average population of prisons, Borstals and detention centres was no less than 35,000. It was 20,000 in the early nineteen-fifties.† Over 9,000 were, in 1968, sleeping two or three in a cell. At the same time prison staffs remain seriously overworked and recruitment is inadequate for a service which has little to commend it to the general public. In such exacting circumstances it is understandable that all is not well, that irregularities occur, and that from time to time serious complaints emerge into public view. Prisoners are sometimes kept in solitary confinement for excessively long periods with privileges withdrawn and even, in one extreme case, the right to attend religious services is reported to have been withheld.

From time to time unusual offenders are put in prison and their reactions when published can exert considerable influence on penal reform. Mrs Bell, the Hampshire magistrate, who spent a short time as an inmate of Holloway as a result of a minor offence which involved her conscience, was amazed by what she saw happening there. She found inmates locked up for up to nineteen hours a day; she endured the utter boredom of the little bit of work she was allowed to do there, and she was shocked by the amount of open lesbianism she witnessed during her brief visit.[17] So, prisons are overcrowded, under-staffed, rife with malpractices which the law itself is supposed to be stamping out, places of boredom and grinding psychological deprivation, yet— and this brings us to the second major fact about them—they have a strikingly low reconviction rate. Something like 85 per cent of men and women who are first committed to gaol do not return to prison again.‡ This might seem, on the face of it, to be a vindication of the

---

* The figure, having reached a record 40,000 in the early nineteen-seventies, had fallen by 1973 to about 38,000—still a very substantial total.
† Pre-1939 the figure was round about 10,000.
‡ At any one time there are some thirty men in prisons or Borstals to every female.

effectiveness of the treatment meted out there but, on further analysis, this proves not to be the case. As Hugh Klare wrote:

> Statistics show that roughly four out of five first offenders do not offend again, no matter what sentence is imposed. Whatever their crime, and whatever their punishment, they have in common their trial which rips away a mask and exposes their weakness and their failure to the public. I believe that those who succeed in re-establishing themselves also share precisely this strong desire to belong to a society whose goodwill they have not only just lost but hope to win again.[18]

It seems fair to deduce from the available evidence that a high proportion of the 'star' prisoners who never return again would have turned out in precisely the same way had they been treated by some other method, and that in their case the high cost and the personal stigma attached to a prison sentence are both economically and socially undesirable. Probation, use of suspended sentences and similar non-institutional procedures would have produced the required result in more acceptable ways. As far as the fifteen to twenty per cent prison failures go the picture is almost equally bleak. It seems that once an individual has embarked on a life of crime or has got into antisocial habits, prison is not very successful in changing his attitude and behaviour. Indeed, some evidence suggests that the experience of being incarcerated is itself powerfully criminogenic and that elements in the experience, far from establishing 'in them the will to lead a good and useful life on discharge', as the Prison Rules 1949 put it, can have exactly the opposite effect.

## Prisonization

Clemmer has been a pioneer in our understanding of the nature of the prison community and with the analysis of what actually goes on inside penal institutions and its bearing on the differential responses of inmates to the experience.[19] His work, and that of Gresham Sykes[20] and the Morrises[21] in this country, has been of considerable value in explaining the differential response rates of the two main groups we have been considering. Clemmer has developed a concept which he calls 'prisonization' which goes a long way towards helping us to appreciate the detrimental effects of serving a prison sentence when a man has already got a record behind him and is in process of crossing that significant line which divides the self-acknowledged criminal from the rest of the community. Every prisoner is exposed to prisonization to some degree. From the very first minute he is stripped of his former identity and obliged to become an anonymous member of a servile and subordinate group. He learns a new language; he is forced to wear strange clothes; his communications with the outside world and with his family, if he has one, are curtailed and subject to bureaucratic control; he is subjected to a regime of arbitrary regimentation against which he has very little effective appeal. But above all he is exposed to a cultural milieu which is largely regulated by the other inmates and to which he is obliged to conform to some degree or to suffer further pains of isolation inside the prison; and this inmate-controlled culture is based on the simple formula of 'us against them'. It is organized around the inverted values of the most persistent offenders and long-term inmates of the system, and reinforced by a code of sanctions which the prison staff are often powerless to inhibit. This kind of socialization to the inmate criminal culture of the institution means that, for some of the weaker personalities and also for those who are exposed for long periods to it, their chances of reform are greatly reduced and their likelihood of becoming recidivists proportionately increased.

The minorities who more or less successfully resist the criminal direction of inmate subcultural pressures are usually those with no previous conviction, those who have only short sentences to serve and those committed for non-violent offences. But, as has already been said, it is doubtful if such offenders should ever have been exposed to the rigours and dangers of a prison sentence in the first place. However that may be, we can see that it is not always the case that prisons, Borstals, or detention centres are to be thought of as 'breeding grounds' for further crime. Given a satisfactory classificatory system the good from the bad risks could be more adequately sorted out from the beginning.

It is worth while pointing out that prisonization affects all inmates, prison officers as well as prisoners. All become institutionalized and tend to behave in stereotyped ways which, as far as the ostensible purpose of the prison system is concerned, may prove to be counter-productive and resistant to change.

*Classification*

Classification for adult offenders is much more primitive even than our present system for sorting and selecting juveniles into appropriate treatment categories. However, there are signs of progress, most notably in the building of an entirely new prison at Grendon Underwood based on pioneering work by Norwood East and Hubert and designed to treat offenders whose psychiatric condition, though not psychotic, is serious enough for them to be placed in maximum security under special medical care. Grendon Underwood caters for men and women and boys and girls, each in separate wings. A further new prison has been opened at Blundeston which is receiving a high proportion of offenders convicted of violent crimes. Wakefield has a long record for treating sexual offenders, while group therapy has been tried out at Wormwood Scrubs, Bristol, Swansea and elsewhere, and casework as well as group work is being practised at Blundeston. Various new treatment methods have also been in train at Borstals and will be touched on further in the succeeding chapter. At this point we merely wish to draw attention to the fact that new ideas are constantly entering the prison system from outside and being tentatively tried out in the exacting conditions of a total institutional setting.

In spite of such changes, however, our prison system remains obdurately traditional and massively Victorian in its public image. As one well-known prisoner said after confinement: 'Prisons don't deter. They don't reform. They don't even punish in any sensible way. Provided you are dirty enough, lazy enough, selfish enough and cunning enough, you can slope through any ordinary sentence without more than the minimum torment.'[22] Clearly this is not satisfactory and the service is ripe for overhaul and drastic reformation. But the fuss over the break-outs in 1966 which led to the Mountbatten enquiry and the panic clamp down on freedom of movement within prisons, and the placing of a ridiculously exaggerated priority on security, has probably halted hope of rapid progress for some time to come. The Mountbatten Report urged concentration of Category A prisoners in maximum security conditions where extra-custodial vigilance would be constantly practised.[23] A later report under the chairmanship of Professor Radzinowicz, on the other hand, recommended a policy of dispersal for those long-term prisoners whose names and records are known to the press and the public to such a degree that their escape would prove embarrassing to government and prison service alike.[24] The Prison Department in the end tended to come down in favour of dispersal and as far as we can see this is their present policy. It is certainly more humane and perhaps in the long run wiser than the close concentration of desperate and subtle criminals with all the attendant dangers of explosive outbreaks on their part and jitters on the side of the prison personnel. We have evidence, based on conference motions amongst prison officers, however, that many of them would prefer the Mountbatten policy. Nevertheless, it is now fairly widely felt that it is possible to exaggerate the dangers to society that certain A class offenders at large might constitute: it is equally held that the conditions under which many of them have been kept in recent years are exactly calculated to drive them to the point of madness and to a sense of hopelessness that is morally indefensible in a country which claims to be civilized. Even in the United States, where the penal system is infinitely more savage than Britain's, the notorious Alcatraz has been closed down.

Prison is seen, hence, to be more or less ineffectual with the inadequate type of chronic recidivist, too harsh even for criminals such as the great train robbers to endure, and unnecessary for most first offenders. It is certainly the wrong kind of place in which to keep sex offenders of any kind. Its role in an enlightened penal system is hence probably marginal and we can look forward to the time when prisons have been replaced by other, sometimes non-residential treatment measures, and when the inmate population is more or less confined to traitors and spies and, in the more specialized institutions, those of the criminal and insane groups whose release would lead to the perpetration of further evil crimes. Nobody, I should imagine, would relish the idea of a man like Brady, one of the two found guilty in the Moors murder case in 1966, ever being loosed upon society again. For some few such offenders, then, in our present state of helplessness, prison must remain a condition of life itself.

*After-care*

Compulsory after-care is now attached to ex-inmates of detention centres, Borstals, and to certain categories of ex-prisoners. In the past, voluntary bodies with philanthropic aims such as the Discharged Prisoners' Aid societies played a major part in the service, but now it is a statutory obligation that one service—namely the Probation and After-Care Service—is responsible for all after-care work and supervision. Voluntary help is, however, still of great value and importance, as was seen in 1966 when the National Association for the Care and Resettlement of Offenders (NACRO) was set up to help to involve members of the community in the care of offenders and to co-operate with the Home Office and all other agencies in the general task of rehabilitation.

The importance of an adequate after-care service for both young and older offenders can hardly be exaggerated. Committal to prison or even to Borstal usually involves a double punishment. First, there is the deprivation of liberty and then, on release, comes the perhaps longer punishment in the form of social ostracism and suspicion. We will the former but not the latter. But we permit it, just as we permit the wives and dependants of prisoners fo suffer psychologically and financially while the husband and father is removed and prevented from performing his function in the home. Clearly enough, a second and purely social punishment is against the spirit of the law and must produce further despair in the minds of ex-prisoners and increase the rate of recidivism.

The needs of ex-inmates are succinctly stated as 'a job, a home and a friend', but since so many of the offenders who have 'a record' often lack one or both or even all these things, the community, acting through its social workers, must try to make good the deficiencies. The task is an immense one, as the degree of recidivism for some groups and classes of offenders indicates. After-care, it has often been pointed out, must begin long before a boy is released from Borstal or a prisoner from gaol. The process of rehabilitation ought, in theory, to commence on the day of admission and go on after the individual has left the institution for a long enough period to enable him to settle down securely. To do this effectively the after-care officer needs to have (and now in fact has) early access to the institution so as to be able to work in close touch with the new welfare officers in the prisons, whose job it is to make preparation for prisoners' after-care. It is important that the offender himself is not regarded by social workers inside and outside the institution as a mere cypher in the organization of his own future life.

Before the mid-nineteen-sixties no part of the penological process had been more neglected than after-care, possibly because legislators were loth to be seen as spending public money on those whom society had chosen to punish. From 1966 the Probation Service was made responsible for the supervision and after-care of all adult prisoners subject to compulsory supervision, and in 1968, additionally, for all prisoners released under the parole scheme. By this time concern at the mounting numbers in prison had strengthened the case for improved after-care as a counter to recidivism, and probation committees were encouraged to allow their officers to devote more time and resources to strengthening contacts with individual prisoners and their families. The integration of what has come to be called 'through care' has been greatly aided by the increased presence in prisons of probation officers, seconded as Prison Welfare Officers, and the Probation and After-Care Service has generally been able to devote more of its capacities to work with these more serious offenders as its commitment to juvenile delinquents has been lessened. The employment of volunteer associates has also increased over the years, and the prison authorities are helpful in ensuring that these public spirited individuals have suitable access to the inmates they have befriended. There has been some fall in the number of committals to prison, and this reduction of pressure on prison staff and the improved after-care system creates a more favourable situation than has ever existed before.

# New trends in methods and treatment 8

In this chapter we will examine various features of the present penal set-up which appear to be growth points for the future. We will also look briefly at various criminological ideas, some of which seem impracticable at the moment while others are shortly, in some shape or form, to be put into effect or have already been experimented with selectively. We have already suggested that better sentencing policy depends upon greater use of magistrates' and judges' classificatory powers, and there have been some important attempts made in recent years to assist towards the solution of these problems by way of predictive devices.

*Police liaison officers*

A comparatively minor experiment which in recent years has roused considerable discussion and one which clearly has links with current thinking in the treatment of younger delinquents, was the development of police juvenile liaison officer schemes. The first one to be established in this country was in Liverpool and began as long ago as 1949. In essence the scheme is an extension of the old practice of administering a police caution at a local bridewell instead of proceeding to court prosecution in the case of children who have not erred greatly and who seem to be more in need of a little homely discipline. Juvenile officers were attached to a police division with high juvenile crime rates, and devoted their whole time to making contact with institutions in the area and establishing liaison with various social workers, ministers of religion and school teachers so that, in the event of a child being reported committing an offence, they had a sound knowledge of the neighbourhood and the resources that could be called upon in an attempt to keep the child out of further trouble. Juvenile liaison officers dealt only with minor and first offenders, with marginal delinquents and children reported to them as being in special need of help and supervision. Schools and local shops were common sources of recruitment, although some children were reported by parents. Supervision lasted for about a year and involved home visits, and attempts, among other things, to help the child make better use of his leisure and to avoid dangerous associates. It is clear that a certain degree of authority entered into the relationship and that the juvenile liaison officer relied upon old-fashioned methods of advice and did not attempt a casework approach. The scheme inevitably aroused some anxiety in its early days, particularly on the part of magistrates who interpreted such intervention by the police as an invasion of their own particular province. School teachers, on the other hand, seem to have welcomed the scheme from its inception and to have made considerable use of the officers in dealing with minor and early delinquency arising within the school itself. Further support is evident in the fact that several other police districts in England and Wales followed Liverpool's example and set up their own juvenile liaison officer service. By 1962, schemes were operating in Leeds, Huddersfield, Birmingham, Bristol, Manchester and Cardiff amongst others, and the Ingleby Committee Report on Children and Young Persons in 1960 commented on the pioneer work in Liverpool and gave it official but rather lukewarm approval. J.L.O. schemes, however, continued without becoming general throughout the police service, and most of the chief constables concerned have reported some degree of success. If we may take the Liverpool experience as not untypical, we find that in the years 1952–9 inclusively 3,572 juveniles were dealt with, of whom only 8 per cent later committed offences. Such satisfactory results probably derive to some extent from the fact that only early and minor delinquents were treated by the scheme, but they also add substance to the claim that is often made that children drifting into bad social habits only need a modicum of care and supervision to bring them back on to an even keel, and that much more dramatic and expensive intervention in many such cases is not only unnecessary but could possibly prove to be positively dangerous by encouraging a child to think of himself as a delinquent rather than as a naughty boy. Since the implementation of the 1969 Children and Young Persons Act the function of the J.L.O.s has changed considerably. Their main task now is to collaborate with the local authority social workers in deciding which children should be cautioned, and which dealt with at court level. In the case of children cautioned some are thought to be in need of further supervision, and the J.L.O.s can and do assist both probation officers and local authority social workers with this task. To some people this may seem to diminish the importance of the J.L.O.s' contribution to the early treatment and prevention of juvenile delinquency but, however that may turn out to be so in the future, the growth of liaison officer services undoubtedly helped to improve the public image of the police at a time when their general effectiveness required all the support they could legitimately muster.

## Prediction

Research into prediction is mainly motivated by the hope that it will some day be possible to achieve something like a scientific penological system, fitting each offender with some degree of confidence to a specific form of treatment. Any predictive instrument which is to serve this end needs to be simple, efficient, reliable and valid if it is ever to survive in the bustle and palaver of modern criminal courts, although most authorities would agree that even a rudimentary predictive formula would be better than the rule of thumb, trial-and-error methods currently in operation.

A predictive equation is fairly simple to understand even for the unmathematically minded. The predictive instrument will depend for its accuracy and usefulness upon the quality of the information put into it and this, in its turn, depends upon our skill in discovering from past experience which factors seem to be more closely associated with success than others. In this way we get over the troublesome notion of the causes of crime and for practical purposes retain the idea that certain factors (for reasons which may be quite unknown or, at best, only partially understood) are reasonably satisfactory indicators of future events and behaviour—although, of course, since we are only dealing in probabilities, not certainties, it will not be possible to be completely sure which group any individual finally ends up in, i.e. whether or not he is to be one of the failures or one of the successes. All we can say with any degree of confidence is that, given the information available, Mr X looks very probably as though he will turn out to be a success when exposed to a particular treatment. Since insurance companies work upon similar actuarial criteria without going bankrupt too often, we can assume that the same method could be applied in the penological field.

The name of Leslie Wilkins has in Britain been closely associated with research into the viability of prediction, and his best known work, carried out in conjunction with Herman Mannheim, was in connection with suitability for Borstal training.[2] This pioneer study began with a thorough analysis of the existing case records of Borstal detainees whose post-release histories were already known. From these records they produced a predictive instrument which made use of a small number of factors called predictors which they knew to be statistically associated with success in Borstal training. Their final list of predictors boiled down to such items as evidence of drunkenness, number of prior offences, absence from home, frequency of job change, and living in a highly industrial area. When this predictive technique was applied to some 338 Borstal inmates, and the results compared with the boys' ultimate performance and also with their housemasters' and governors' forecasts for them, it was found to be much more accurate than the latter and was, in fact, valid for 212 of the total case studies. When it is remembered that the researchers were working without any personal knowledge of the boys or contact with them, and that they were basing their predictions solely upon the existing case records (which would almost certainly be unstandardized and originally compiled for quite different purposes), the outcome of the project is most impressive.

In America, Sheldon and Eleanor Glueck, following upon Ernest Burgess's earlier pioneering work, have also experimented with the preparation of a prediction table derived from their long term studies of five hundred delinquent boys and their non-delinquent controls.[3] Of their three tables the one called Social Prediction is of widest potential application. In its simplified form this reduces predictive data to five categories, *viz.* discipline of boy by father (lax, firm and kindly, or over-strict and erratic); supervision of boy by mother (unsuitable, fair or suitable); affection of father for boy (indifferent or hostile, or warm, including over-protective); affection of mother for boy; and, finally, cohesiveness of family (unintegrated, some elements of cohesion or cohesive). All assessments were based on the judgement of social workers, but in spite of possible variability between them the Gluecks claim that they have produced a valuable device capable of wide application and of further refinement. Some follow-up studies seem to support this claim and these have been listed and discussed by Professor Glueck in several papers and books.

In Britain Dr D. H. Stott has also worked for some considerable time endeavouring to produce a simple device which could be used by teachers and social workers to pick out those children who are high delinquency risks. His study of four-hundred-odd Glasgow boys aged eight to fifteen who were put on probation in 1957 and their performance compared with a 'matched' control group of similarly situated boys, all of whom were assessed by his own Bristol Social Adjustment Guide, enabled him in the end to produce a very simple sorting device which would take from ten to fifteen minutes for a teacher or social worker to apply.[4] He further refined this device to the point that the teacher would only need to answer 'yes' or 'no' to six questions framed to cover the spectrum of 'delinquency-prone behaviour-disturbance'. Should the answer to any of the questions be 'yes', then the more thorough schedule of questions would be used as outlined in the Bristol Social Adjustment Guide. Stott claims that, had such a method been applied to his group of Glasgow probationers, it might have accurately detected no less than three-quarters of high delinquency risks.

The rationale of prediction is clear enough. If we could only spot children with delinquent proclivities before they commit their offences we might conceivably save them from ever falling foul of the law, perhaps by giving them and their parents additional support and by providing facilities lacking in the environment. Furthermore, predictive formulae which would suggest what forms of treatment are likely to be successful with particular kinds of offenders, and even negatively, what treatments are likely to be unsuccessful, would give considerable help to judges and magistrates in developing a surer, more uniform and rational sentencing policy. Further follow up studies, however, of the precise outcomes of treatments in many individual cases would be necessary to check up on the continuing validity of such prescriptive predictions. Finally, predictive measures could be very helpful in selecting candidates for parole and might save a great deal of the time and energies of parole boards and committees and, indeed, prove to be much more accurate. Lloyd Ohlin has described an interesting start in the state of Illinois with what he calls, perhaps more properly, 'Experience Tables' and, on the whole, he is optimistic regarding the future use and long-term value of such methods.[5]

There are no indications that prediction is likely to be widely applied in Britain, however. The Home Office has apparently made limited use of the Mannheim-Wilkins method with somewhat ambiguous results and lessening reliability. Research is continuing in the juvenile field where there is a growing emphasis on prevention rather than on cure, but to date there does not seem to have been any substantial use made of the ideas and techniques advocated by Dennis Stott. This does not mean, however, that the notion of spotting the delinquency-prone child will never be accepted and employed. It is merely that, in Britain at least, we are very slow to adopt new ideas or to use any procedures in the treatment of delinquents which have a scientific and impersonal basis and which many people see as 'cold blooded'. When the idea of prevention gets firmer hold and after the new legislation based on the white paper *Children in Trouble* is securely established, it may become more acceptable, and be considered no more damaging to be regarded as delinquency-prone than it is at the present time to have a below average I.Q. or a tendency to asthma or epileptic fits.

Although our penal attitudes tend to be ultra-conservative, growing uneasiness over existing methods and procedures is apparent

## Group work

The development of group-work methods in some prisons and Borstals is a good example of the way in which ideas invade the penal system from outside and become partially assimilated to the system to produce minor modifications which may nevertheless prove to be important turning points for the future. Group work has been practised in British penal institutions since 1958 along the lines laid down by Dr Fenton in the state prisons of California.[6] In 1962 the Prison Commissioners issued their first official statement which outlined the aims of group work and so gave it increased status and recognition. Four years later the Prison Department published a booklet called *Group Work in Prisons and Borstals 1962-6*, which comprised a series of articles written by different authors which described what had been achieved so far and essayed some kind of assessment of results.[7]

Group counselling is practised in small groups of some eight inmates who meet regularly in the company of a member of staff 'to discuss in an informal atmosphere any subject they wish'. Meetings are usually weekly and of an hour and a half's duration. No records are kept and, theoretically at least, no topic is barred, but complete confidentiality cannot be guaranteed. Staff members who take groups meet together as a group to discuss their experiences with a group counselling supervisor (usually a deputy or assistant governor), the advisor and sometimes the governor himself. Advisors are normally drawn from the ranks of the prison service psychologists who have received some form of special training for the job. As an outsider it is difficult to know what goes on in these group sessions, but the claim is made that they are broadly therapeutic and aim 'to help to correct, in some degree, the distorted view which many inmates have of themselves and of society, and which is often responsible for the behaviour that has brought them into conflict with the law'.[8] At the moment we have no way of assessing such a claim objectively, but the Prison Department state that 'it is the undoubted fact that many inmates are brought by this method to see a truer picture of themselves and their behaviour as a member of society'.[9] What is clear, however, is that this kind of group counselling and guided discussion, as of course it must be, is not to be equated with psychiatric treatment.

In spite of the unsupported claim that group methods are effective with some inmates, the authors of the pamphlet go on to make a much humbler case for their usefulness. They say that the Commissioners place great value on the fact that staff and inmates can meet in this way as human beings and relate to each other more naturally. Staff who are admittedly seen 'only as figures of authority' assume a new and much more flexible role which is probably all to the good when they each and every one return to their more formal roles in the normal system. It is likely at the moment, at least, that such sessions do no harm to the inmates and that they do some positive good to the staff who participate since they receive special training for the work and are thereby enabled to acquire greater understanding of the sociological and psychological forces operating within their institution. Moreover, by involving prison officers in treatment, much of the old bitterness between those giving treatment and those with merely custodial duties will be modified and possibly eliminated. There is no evidence that reconviction rates for ex-prisoners who have received group counselling are any lower than for those who have not. There is, however, a chance that if all inmates become involved in such counselling the whole basis of prison as it now exists will come in for angry criticism, and that resentments against authoritarianism will reach explosion point. In other words, the values implicit in group counselling do not fit easily and happily into the regime of a total penal institution in which arbitrary control is necessarily involved for ninety per cent of the time. Before counselling can have a fair chance of success and be truly incorporated as part of a therapeutic programme, the whole nature of prisons, as such, and even of Borstals to a rather lesser degree, will have to be transformed. At the moment group work is mainly marginal to the system and its use largely to be interpreted as a tentative step towards developing a kind of casework within a group setting (rather than on a one-to-one basis), and the policy is so far to confine it to inmates of selected institutions.

## Half-way houses and hostels

It has often been pointed out that the change from having one's life almost entirely organized by others in a total institution to being free of all but the normal social restraints and more or less left to one's own resources after discharge is too great for some of the weaker and more inadequate ex-detainees to sustain. In the free-for-all of ordinary everyday life they may feel lost and helpless. If they have no family to return to or no job to take up they are all the more rootless and confused and so likely to commit further crimes. We know that it is the first six months after discharge that is crucial, that failure to settle down during the early weeks after release is most common amongst habitual offenders, and, as we have already seen in connection with ex-Borstal boys, those without homes to return to have the highest reconviction rates. Hence, attempts have been made to bridge the gap between prison and the outside world in several ways. First by providing within the walls a special hostel where prisoners due to be discharged can live in much more normal conditions than is possible within the ordinary prison building.\* This kind of transitional community is especially designed to help long-term offenders get their civilian feet, as it were, before final discharge. As far as possible those in the hostels attached to prisons go out to work and obtain short-term employment in the surrounding locality during the last six months of their sentence. They draw their wages like ordinary men, pay towards their upkeep, and save something against the day of their release. The second kind of hostel is designed to meet the needs of detainees after discharge and is run by voluntary agencies. Probably the best known of these is Norman House which did outstanding pioneering work with the care of

\* Some of these hostels have been closed—apparently for security reasons—since the Mountbatten enquiry and report.

homeless, persistent offenders.[10] Its first warden, Mervyn Turner, has become widely recognised as an expert on the needs of this kind of chronic offender who cannot be allowed for his own good to drift back into normal social life but who needs the continuing support of friendly, non-judgemental and stable social workers within an atmosphere of unregimented order. Many more hostels on the Norman House model (there are three at present) are obviously needed to cope with the rising number of ex-prisoners, and some could very usefully be developed in conjunction with organized after-care.

The special needs of some ex-Borstal boys are also being met by a most promising experimental hostel, Northways, in the London area. Dr Derek Miller has been closely associated with its work and has written its first report.[11] Only a small number of boys can be helped by this hostel's mildly permissive regime which is flexible and sympathetic without giving the boys the idea that the staff could be used as doormats. Boys in the hostel go out to work and live quite normal lives but have adults to relate to in a realistic way and the discipline of communal living to accept and come to terms with. It appears to be most successful with boys who are not suffering from severe mental illness. By comparison with a control group of ex-Borstal boys in different environmental conditions, the Northways group showed that they had a better chance of not being reconvicted during a two-year follow-up period. It seems likely that if only similar hostels could be made more widely available then the recidivism of homeless ex-Borstal boys too could be greatly reduced, and it would appear to be a sensible policy for the Home Office itself to initiate, but probably not actually to run, a number of Northways in other parts of the country.

## *Parole*

The most recent major innovation in the British penal system is the introduction of a modified version of parole as practised by various other countries for some considerable time. The Criminal Justice Act 1967 inaugurated the scheme which was first operational in April the following year. According to the Act, prisoners become eligible for parole when they have served a third of their sentences or a year, whichever is longer. It is effectively restricted to prisoners serving more than eighteen months, for those serving a determinate sentence are released at the two-thirds point of sentence if they obtain full remission; if serving less than eighteen months they are not in prison long enough to qualify. Something in the region of 5,000 men and women prisoners were eligible before a rigorous weeding out process was carried through by specially constituted local review committees made up of prison personnel, probation officers and visiting magistrates. Suitability for release on parole is gauged by a number of factors such as a prisoner's previous record and response to training, plus his prospects of a job to go to and an assessment of his home background. The Parole Board not unexpectedly erred on the side of caution in the early months in order not to arouse adverse publicity for the new scheme. Even so, the Home Office initially rejected a considerable number of cases which had been recommended by the local review committees and referred to the Board only such recommended cases as appeared to be good parole prospects. The original release rate of only 8·5 per cent of those eligible attracted much informed criticism. Subsequently the Home Secretary acceded to strong representations from the Board that he should refer to them all cases which had been favourably recommended by the local review committees. As a result the number of prisoners released on parole increased significantly between 1968 and 1970. Later, agreement was reached to send to the Board a selection of cases not recommended, and in 1972 over 1,000 such cases had been referred, of whom 26 per cent received parole. From 1 January 1973 the Home Secretary has been empowered to release on licence certain categories of offenders on the recommendations of the local review committees and without special reference to the Board; this recognizes the contribution of the local review committees and is an indication of the large measure of agreement between the decisions of these committees and the Board.

In 1972 the Board considered a total of 4,593 cases of whom 4,450 were determinate sentences. Of this number 2,926 were recommended for parole; the Home Secretary felt unable to agree with the

Board in only 11 instances. There were 143 prisoners serving life sentences who were considered and 54 were recommended as suitable for release on licence about a year ahead, subject to good behaviour in the meantime; the Home Secretary was unable to accept 9 such recommendations. The average parole period is now around 8 months, and there are about 1,550 on parole at any time.

Parole supervision makes a heavy demand on a probation officer's time and attention. He must maintain contact with a prisoner and his family during the period of sentence, and provide up-to-date reports on the home situation when the prisoner becomes eligible for parole and for each subsequent review if the need arises. He helps the prisoner with a release plan which may well involve a delicate intervention in complicated relationships as well as the more usual arrangements for suitable work and accommodation on discharge. Many ex-inmates of prisons and Borstals are homeless, however, and present special problems, but the greater provision of after-care hostels has been of great assistance in this respect.

There has been a very recent reduction in the prison population and there is a prospect that this trend will continue. This very welcome development may stem from the increased resort to parole, which reduces the numbers held in prison, and from the use of other non-custodial measures made possible by the Criminal Justice Act 1972.\* Deferment of sentence and an increased use of probation hostels for adults may also influence the situation. The hard pressed probation service stands at the centre of all these provisions to avoid custodial treatment of offenders, or to lessen the time spent in custody. It is important that the probation officer on whom so much now depends should be given the fullest support in the very responsible work he undertakes.

The parole system can now be said to have proved itself as a valuable addition to penological practice in this country. It can still be criticised, for example, on the lapse of time between the first interview by a local review committee member and the eventual decision of the Board, or for the absence of explanation of reasons

---

\* See pp. 130-32 below.

for the refusal of parole; but it is evident that the Board is a vigorous and independent body eager to ensure that the prison custody of an offender gives way to responsible supervision in the open as soon as it is commensurate with public interest.

## Suspended Sentences

Suspended sentences were introduced in Britain in 1967, in an attempt to reduce the numbers of people serving prison sentences, and became operative the following year. Under the provisions of the Act the imposition of a suspended sentence was mandatory on the courts for offenders who would have incurred a six-month sentence, and discretionary for those guilty of offences involving imprisonment for up to two years. The reformist theory argued that this would lead to a reduction in the number of people serving prison sentences, but the facts proved otherwise. Magistrates made too frequent use of the suspended sentence order as a kind of caution for comparatively minor offences, with the result that anyone who was unlucky enough to be convicted of two such offences, neither of which alone would have been deemed serious enough for prison sentences to be imposed, found himself incarcerated as a 'man with a record'. The operation of suspended sentencing almost certainly contributed to the rise in the prison population which in 1970 reached record proportions. The manner in which this policy was conceived and more or less uncritically applied is an example of how unscientific zeal can sometimes prove to be counter-productive. It is one thing to introduce suspended sentencing in countries which have no alternatives to prison but quite another to employ it in a country like Britain which already has a number of useful and well-established alternatives available to the courts. Conditional discharge and probation were already capable of achieving all that might be gained by suspended sentencing and would not, even when unsuccessful, necessarily have led to more people being sent to prison. It is clearly erroneous to imagine that by adding to the battery of alternative sentences to imprisonment we are bound to reduce the prison population, if only indeed for the fact that now, as in the past, a prison sentence is the ultimate sanction which lies behind all efforts to correct law-breakers.

Amending legislation passed in the Criminal Justice Act of 1972, which removed the obligation to impose suspended sentences in certain cases also seems to be an ill-conceived policy change, since statistics tend to show that it was the mandatory cases which had the highest success, i.e. lower breach, rates. As the Howard League Annual Report 1971-72 said: 'It is time we stopped legislating on the basis of judicial or parliamentary hunches as to the rightness of particular penalties, and introduced changes in a systematic way that would enable their results to be evaluated.'

## Day Training Centres

One of the more hopeful and interesting changes brought about by the Criminal Justice Act 1972 was the institution of Day Training Centre orders for certain categories of known offenders with a history of unemployment and failure and who are deemed to be more inadequate and socially damaged than dangerous to society. By the end of 1973 there were four experimental centres operating in London, Liverpool, Sheffield and Pontypridd, staffed and run by probation officers who are responsible for arranging a sixty-day course of social training which may include, amongst other more recreational activities, remedial teaching, group discussion and individual counselling. The hope is that these men who have already failed to respond to other forms of treatment will now be helped to readjust their mental attitudes to the community and to the problem of getting a job and earning their own living, and so cease to be a burden on the rest of society. First offenders are not eligible for day training centre orders nor, in the first instance, are 'hardened recidivists', alcoholics, drug addicts or those with diagnosed mental illnesses. The main drive of the programme at these centres is to revive self-discipline and personal pride in those who have so far found it more comfortable to evade the challenges of life by docile submission to the routines of prison. It is realized that a sixty-day course is not likely to achieve this without continuing effort and support after the official period of attendance is over, and it is hoped that voluntary contact with the probation officers running the centres will be maintained.

It is difficult at this stage to evaluate the chance of success that this new treatment is likely to have. So much indeed depends on individual responsiveness and also upon the availability of suitable employment in the particular area in which the offenders live. The establishment of these centres perhaps springs from a not very realistic faith in the effectiveness of caring concern on the part of the probation officers to undo the long years of self-doubt and inadequacy which, in some cases, may be as much the result of individual short-comings as of social disadvantages. Nevertheless, any attempt to prevent the socially inadequate from the further deterioration that could arise from additional periods of stultifying imprisonment is to be welcomed, and even if, in the event, the success rate proves to be disappointingly low, the effort is undoubtedly justified on general moral and humanitarian grounds.

*Community Service Orders*

Community Service Orders were originally projected in the *Report of the Advisory Council on the Penal System, Non-custodial and Semi-custodial Penalties*, 1970, subsequently known as the Wootton Report. The 1972 Criminal Justice Act introduced compulsory community service into Britain as an experimental penal measure, although it had in a variety of forms already operated in the U.S.A. Offenders who are given C.S.O.s will normally be over seventeen but no particular category is specified in the Act, although anyone given such an order will have committed an imprisonable offence. They will be obliged to undertake approved work in the community such as helping the aged, clearing up derelict sites, assisting in hospitals or at children's playgrounds, undertaking, in fact, as a penalty many forms of community help that voluntary service workers have for many years been performing as a matter of social conscience. The service is administered by the Probation and After-Care Service, although voluntary help is also almost a *sine qua non*. Work will be done during the offender's leisure time, especially at weekends. A maximum of 140 hours is required to be performed. In the event of an offender not carrying out his commitment under the order he may be brought back to court and fined in addition to continuing to do his community service, or he may have another sentence imposed for the original offence.

The experiment has so far (1974) been confined to six selected areas of the country—Inner London, Kent, Shropshire, Durham, Nottinghamshire and South West Lancashire. Results will inevitably be difficult to evaluate, but those who have been involved in the work seem to be optimistic. The Home Office research department is monitoring their progress and achievements and if, on balance, they seem to be having a reasonable degree of success in preventing young men with a number of previous convictions from offending again, they will certainly be extended to other parts of the country. Not only are community service orders comparatively inexpensive as alternatives to institutional treatment, but they also have a genuinely rehabilitative motivation in so far as they require a man to give some form of penitential service to the community he has harmed by his crime. It is hoped that those undergoing C.S.O.s will continue with their community work on a voluntary basis when their order has expired, and become permanently associated with established voluntary social service projects in their neighbourhoods. As in the case of Day Training Centres, Community Service Orders are aimed at preventing more people having to go to prison than is absolutely unavoidable, and they bear witness to the growing spirit of rational reform and clemency which is coming to typify our general approach to the treatment of offenders.

## New policies in child care

We have already touched on the various new policies and methods of treatment which the 1969 Children and Young Persons Act brought about, and we must now look at these changes in more detail and examine their penological significance. There has been a growing desire in the past twenty years or so for a drastic overhaul of existing procedures for coping with young offenders, in the hope that, by placing more emphasis on supporting families and by improving facilities in the community generally, many of the children whom we now stigmatize as criminals might be prevented from becoming delinquents at all. The rationale that underlies such attempts derives from the view that delinquents are essentially deprived children, and that their needs for security and training are not dissimilar from those who are neglected or in need of care or protection but who happen not to have broken the law. This is undoubtedly an attractive view and one that at the moment is widely supported. It leads to the conclusion that prosecution and recourse to the juvenile court is inappropriate for those under sixteen years of age or so, and that they should be dealt with, as happens in various other countries, by welfare committees composed of social workers and child care experts who would propose a form of treatment suitable to a child's needs in a non-punitive, non-legalistic atmosphere.

The notion that all children should be treated alike as basically the responsibility of the family and of educational institutions received strong support from the Scottish committee under the chairmanship of Lord Kilbrandon which reported in 1964.[12] Briefly, the Kilbrandon Committee made the following main recommendations: all juveniles under sixteen who were considered to be in need of care should be dealt with by a specially created non-judicial juvenile panel and, in the case of delinquents, provided the child and his parents agreed, an identical procedure would take place; in disputed cases a sheriff's court would adjudicate and have power upon a finding of guilt to refer the child back to the juvenile panel; in each local authority a Director of Social Education would be appointed to look after child guidance, school medical services, school welfare and attendance, and also the provision of special schools for maladjusted or handicapped children; residential homes and hostels would come under this new authority; and the whole business of coping with children with problems would be fundamentally dealt with as an educational matter.* It is clear that the recommendations of this committee exerted considerable influence south of the border where more conservative views were successfully holding up reform

* These proposals were translated into law by the Social Work (Scotland) Bill of 1968.

and proposing nothing more than a minor tinkering with the existing system. However, the Labour Party's working committee under Lord Longford, which issued its findings in June 1964 in a rush of pre-election campaigning enthusiasm, also advocated an extended family welfare service, and when that party came to power shortly after it was not surprising that their white paper, *The Child, the Family and the Young Offender*,[13] of the following year followed similar lines to those put forward by the Longford and Kilbrandon committees. At that point a country-wide argument between social workers, educators, criminologists and penologists broke out, and so fiercely did the debate flare up, and so hot were the viewpoints expressed, that three years elapsed before the Government eventually printed a new white paper, *Children in Trouble*,[14] which proposed a modified version of its original scheme.

Critics of the first white paper seized on its rather complicated and cumbersome procedures for dealing with offenders and other needy children by a series of graduated stages, with built-in safeguards, which would almost certainly have been difficult for administrators, let alone children and their parents, to understand and apply. Juvenile courts as we now know them would become almost marginal in the proposed new set-up, and welfare committees would be called on to deal with the vast majority of cases up to the age of sixteen. Children under that age having committed an act that would have been an offence for an older person, and those in need of care or protection, would be brought before a local family council whose job it would be to decide on treatment in collaboration with the parents or guardians. In cases of dispute reference would be made to a court for determination. Young offenders' courts for those over sixteen and under twenty-one would also be established along traditional lines. Residential treatment, where judged necessary would, for the under-sixteens, be in local authority children's homes and, for the over-sixteens, in the approved schools which would be taken over and run directly by the Home Office. Arrangements for making social enquiries and for carrying out treatment programmes for the younger age group would be the sole responsibility of children's departments of the local authorities.

Apart from the complexity of the suggestions, critics of the white paper also objected to the fact that legal safeguards involved in the administration of the courts would be removed and that a child could be sent to an approved hostel, involving genuine loss of individual freedom, without any chance to appeal and without due legal protection. Once parents and social workers had agreed on a course of action, the child would have to submit, although one could foresee serious difficulties here since parents and social workers might well disagree strongly in a great many instances. It is difficult to accept the force of these legalistic objections, partly because, for most children, the finding of guilt by the juvenile court is a pure formality, and also because in so many other aspects of life a child is inevitably at the mercy of parents, teachers, social workers and other adults, and it is difficult to see how things could be organized otherwise. A criticism which, in my view, has much more substance results from the loss of contact between the probation service and the under-seven-teens, for probation officers by their training, dedication and traditions are professionally committed to the care of delinquents in a way and to a degree that no other group of social workers can be. It is vital that young delinquents should feel that they have a special adult to whom they can go, and to whom, indeed, they are required to go, and who is solely concerned with their problems. It is doubtful whether generic social workers have such a commitment, and it is debatable whether they will ever be able to do for the young offender all that, in the past, the probation service has done.

The to and fro of public discussion that went on between 1965 and 1968 bore some fruit in a second white paper, *Children in Trouble*, which, as we have said, presents a much modified version of the earlier proposals. This white paper, too, has come in for fierce attack, somewhat on the same lines. Its provisions are, however, embodied in the new legislation and for the next few years even those who disagree with the provisions will be obliged to do the best they can with them. In effect, what we have is an integrated personal social service department on which is placed a massive new burden in the shape of dealing with all delinquents under the age of fourteen as social welfare cases, and for deciding with the police, in respect of the fourteens to seventeens, which should or should not be brought before the court. All deprived children up to fourteen receive identical treatment to the erstwhile delinquents. The emphasis in the future will be increasingly laid upon prevention, early diagnosis of difficulty, and widely based community and casework care. Provision of what is termed 'intermediate treatment'† will replace the work hitherto carried out by junior attendance centres and junior detention centres. The new intermediate treatment is of particular interest and promise since it involves making use of children's free time when they will be obliged to take part in organized recreation (possibly on youth club lines) or social service or adventure training (on Outward Bound lines), the aim being to bring the young person into contact with different social influences and endeavour to secure his participation in constructive activities which will be of social value and will not, in themselves, be perceived as punitive so much as retributive in character. Children requiring treatment away from home are placed in the care of the local authority in what are now called 'community homes'. These include a wide range of establishments incorporating the work previously done by remand homes, reception centres, L.E.A. homes and hostels, approved schools and some voluntary homes. In due course Borstal sentences for those under seventeen will cease to exist and children going to community homes will do so as a result of a supervision order made out in the name of the local authority social work department.

Under the 1969 Act the juvenile courts have been retained but their powers have been considerably curtailed. A child is now brought before the court only if he has committed an offence and is also thought to be in need of care and control. Otherwise he will receive a police caution if he is considered to come from a 'good' home. There is thus some degree of social bias involved in the way in which juveniles are processed. This has led to legal controversy but it is the reduced power of the courts which has produced greater argument and concern. The only course open to magistrates for a child

† Regional planning departments set up by the Department of Health and Social Security are now responsible for designating various schemes as being suitable for intermediate treatment.

below the age of fourteen who offends is to commit him to the care of the local authority, and this they must do however many times he breaks the law. It is the sole responsibility of the local authority's social workers to decide whether or not any more drastic action than supervision is required, e.g. committal to a community home or a requirement to accept intermediate treatment. Some magistrates have complained publicly about the number of occasions juveniles have been brought before them for offences for which they feel themselves now impotent to deal. As far as the over-fourteens go, however, a detention centre order may still be made out, and for the over-fifteens committal to a Borstal is available. Hence there is at the present time a dramatic switch from a fairly mild and remedial to a much more punitive approach at the age of fourteen-plus which has little logic to justify it.

There are hence highly controversial features in the 1969 Act which time and experience will no doubt help to rectify by subsequent amendments. But there are also possible long-term gains, notably in the full and final eradication of a purely penal attitude towards youngsters who fall foul of the law, and an attempt to replace such concepts with more humane and dignified forms of treatment in line with the values of a truly caring community.

All this, of course, will take a considerable time to be fully implemented. Something like a decade will probably pass before substantial institutional changes become apparent, before old ideas and attitudes are outmoded and an adequate number of suitably qualified social workers are recruited effectively to put into practice the social ideals that underpin the whole exercise.

# Conclusion 9

In the foregoing chapters we have looked in some detail at sociocultural interpretations of the meaning of crime and we have examined various sociological theories regarding causation. We have also looked at the statistical facts and tried to discover significant trends; finally, we undertook a bird's eye survey of existing procedures for dealing with offenders and produced what evidence is available regarding their effectiveness.

*Criminological theory*

We can sum up most of the important theories about urban delinquency in a series of propositions which sometimes overlap and sometimes even appear to be contradictory.[1]
1. Crime is a predominantly urban phenomenon and in comparatively small, static and homogeneous rural areas crime rates are low.
2. Criminal statistics suggest that crime is closely associated with lower-class neighbourhoods. It has a strong subcultural basis and is a reaction on the part of depressed groups against social and economic frustrations imposed on them by more successful and more powerful classes.
3. Crime is part and parcel of a special way of life which has grown up in lower-class and economically poor neighbourhoods and is intimately associated with the *positive* cultural values of such localities. Homogeneous slum neighbourhoods encourage juvenile gangs and so perpetuate a delinquent tradition independently of middle-class culture and institutions.
4. Crime is unevenly distributed even amongst lower-status groups, all of whom might be expected to react against social and economic

frustrations with equal force. Differential delinquency rates are to be found amongst people living in the same kind of locality and in the same broad occupational class.
5. Crime is often closely associated with rooming house districts. But in some cities the latter have lower crime rates than the old closer-knit slum neighbourhood.
6. The quality of home life and family relationships seem to be crucial in deciding whether or not a child becomes delinquent.
7. Where there is stability in social relationships and where the local community is homogeneous in culture and belief, delinquency is less common and vice versa. The delinquency rate is a measure of the existence of *anomie*, and where there is an absence of agreed standards of behaviour and little social cohesion it is more frequently to be found.
8. The social isolation of problem families is conducive to child delinquency.
9. Crime is found throughout the entire social order. Offences committed by professional people or by businessmen are usually associated with their occupational roles. They are often undetected or, even if detected, dealt with outside the courts. Upper- and middle-class juveniles are frequently treated informally by teachers and parents.

An attempt must now be made to see how far these propositions are essentially contradictory and to what extent they may be reconciled in a general theory of criminal and delinquent behaviour.

The ecological distribution of high crime rates amongst people living in older and poorer areas might partly arise, it seems reasonable to suppose, because of the experience of discrimination arising from the residents' lowly occupational and economic roles. This may engender feelings of animosity. It would also certainly make detection and subsequent prosecution a much less serious experience. A history of poverty and overcrowding coupled with lowly status could further produce a kind of family life which lacks effective supervision and control of children, and this, in turn, could lead to the growth of gangs and delinquent groups in search of excitement and willing to indulge in various kinds of hooliganism and larceny.

Such a view, which is, in effect, an amalgamation of the Cohen-Cloward and Ohlin and the Morris-Miller-Mays theories, would also be reconcilable with the psychological hypotheses, viz. that maladjusted children living in areas where delinquent traditions already exist could utilize these traditional modes of behaviour through which to express their internal strife. Problem families, especially those which are socially isolated, create delinquency amongst their children as a by-product of familial malfunctioning. Such children steal because they are unhappy, unsupervised and inadequately disciplined.

Rooming house districts which *per se* consist of many socially disconnected households are similarly conducive to *anomie* and produce a delinquent crop in proportion to their lack of cohesiveness.

We, therefore reach a position where we see that homogeneity *both* produces *and* inhibits delinquency. Where there is a group feeling of underprivilege and where there is a local tradition for certain kinds of delinquency in existence, homogeneity fosters anti-social behaviour. But homogeneity works against criminality in areas where there are strong cultural uniformities, for example amongst Jewish and Chinese communities, in cases, in fact, where there is a strong family spirit and commitment to a particular way of life and belief.[2]

Similarly, *anomie* (the absence of agreed norms) works in both directions. Inadequate isolated families find it hard to prevent their offspring breaking the law. Large areas in which there are confused and conflicting values, for example, cosmopolitan city centres, also encourage illegal behaviour. Families, however, with strong internal cohesion and loyalty, even in criminogenic areas, effectively stand out against the delinquent content of the local culture. Such families are, in terms of their local milieu, socially disconnected, or, if we want to use another word, non-conforming.

We have now accounted, in general terms, for the different kinds of delinquent behaviour and motivation hypothesized by Cohen, Cloward and Ohlin, Harriet Wilson, Morris, Mays, Sprott, Downes and various other criminologists. All can be brought under the even wider umbrella of the Shaw-Burgess-McKay concept of the delinquency area. Delinquency areas are lower-class; they can be *either* homogeneous or characterized by *anomie*, close-knit *or* socially disconnected. Each kind of lower-class locality can contribute its little quantum to the total delinquency bill. In none is delinquency inevitable, however. The quality of home life and family relationships can withstand the adverse social pressures in individual cases, although it is only likely to do this in substantial numbers when there is a fairly solid cultural or religious or ethnic community to give the individual members of the family the requisite support.

Middle-class and white-collar crime is, by contrast, not locality-based to any degree. As far as adults go, the kinds of offences which the higher status and income groups are most likely to commit are ones fairly closely associated with the workplace rather than with the home territory. The kinds of offence that middle-class youngsters commit may be similar to those poorer-class children commit, i.e. damage to property, petty theft, etc., but they tend, in the main, to be dealt with not as crimes, but as childish indiscipline. Home and school combine to treat such peccadilloes as matters of private concern and either of school or family discipline.

If this analysis is in broad measure true, it would account for the preponderance of lower-class individuals in official crime statistics. It would prevent us, too, falling into the error of assuming that lower-class people are more criminalistic than others. Their predominance in official statistics is, to some extent, merely a reflection of their lower social status. In so far as certain individuals are congenitally stress-prone, the experience of being brought up in a frustrating and socially depressed environment is likely to exacerbate the fundamental susceptibility to psycho-social maladjustment. Furthermore, the kinds of crimes they commit are often unsophisticated and thus more likely to be found out. Their occupational roles expose them more to simple direct theft than to embezzlement or other kinds of financial fiddling. Moreover, when middle-class parents break the law they do so in ways that are unknown to and unavailable to their children and thus they cannot provide the kind of delinquent model that, perhaps, manual workers may sometimes provide for their offspring. Better off people are also possibly less tempted by the rewards of petty theft, and more likely to lose their status and income if found out. They experience, then, something of a social disincentive to commit minor delinquencies, although major crime may still appeal to them.

We may, perhaps, catch a glimpse of the differential treatment handed out to youngsters from different social backgrounds if we think of the ways in which college students behave on recognized rag days. Often they commit acts of violence and even of vandalism which, had they been committed down town by working-class youths on any ordinary day of the week, would result in police arrest and conviction at court. Even if apprehended, a child from a so-called 'good' home is often dismissed with a caution, whereas a child from a so-called 'bad' home is much more likely to be placed on probation or dealt with in an apparently more severe manner.

In summary, then, we may say that, while delinquency and law-breaking are something to which all are exposed in modern urban society, and while both social influences and personal psychological problems operate in all sections of the community, those who are most likely to become the subjects of official proceedings are much more likely to be those who derive from lower-status homes and follow lower-grade occupations. Any research, therefore, which is mainly based upon court cases will miss the complex subtleties of criminal behaviour and tend, however unwittingly, to perpetuate the widely held view that delinquency is predominantly a lower-class phenomenon. It could hence operate as a kind of self-fulfilling prophecy and so prove to be seriously and permanently misleading. A study based on official figures, then, tells us as much about the nature of our society and about the way justice is administered as about the true nature of delinquency in the human mind and heart.

## Criminological theory and penal practice

One would now wish to put together the two main parts of the essay, i.e. the theoretical and the practical, to see if they complement each other and make sense. It seems to be especially important, in view of ever rising crime rates and the expense involved in dealing with criminals and delinquents, to see how far present and proposed methods of treatment mesh in with current theories and research findings.

One fact should by now be transparently clear: crime and delinquency are highly complex socio-legal and psychological phenomena, and since they refer to behaviour which runs the spectrum from benign to malignant, normal to abnormal, our understanding is likely to remain at a primitive level for some time to come. This, of course, does not excuse stagnation in treatment or administration and we have a responsibility to utilize what little knowledge we have gained as sagaciously as possible.

We know that crime is probably still increasing. We believe that it is endemic. We also know that many of our traditional methods for containing and treating it are ineffectual and seem to be becoming more so. At the same time we know that the life-long criminal career is exceptional and that, statistically speaking, the greater proportion of all offences are committed by ordinary common-or-garden individuals very much like ourselves, if, indeed, we are lucky enough not to be numbered amongst the known offenders. We can therefore begin a rudimentary classification by seeking ways to distinguish the serious from the less serious social risks. If we consider the case of James Griffiths who, at the age of thirty-four, was shot dead by Glasgow police in July 1969 while resisting arrest on a charge of murder, having already wounded thirteen other people by gunshot before he was slain like some old-time Chicago gangster, we can see how the tangled and complex inter-relationship of personality disorder, social background and penal institutionalization produces the ultimate tragedy with all the inevitability of classical Greek drama. All the ingredients are there: stealing habits and recalcitrance before ten years of age, brought to court as beyond parental control, shopbreaking, theft, approved school, probation, psychiatric treatment, army experience which excited an interest in guns, followed by imprisonment, robbery with violence and, in the end, murder. To pigeon-hole such a man as a psychopath takes us no further in understanding why the community at a much earlier stage did not intervene in his developing life cycle. But clearly it is in the prevention and treatment of such tough and dangerous offenders that the main weight of our penal services should be directed. At the present moment the police and other agencies spend too much of their time on a great number of juveniles whose offences are persistent but petty, and upon a smaller group of chronic recidivists who are more pathetic than menacing.

The discipline and guidance of children from the earliest stages of delinquency or kindred difficulty would seem to be wise social policy and this has now at last come to be seen as a mainly educational problem. Children who have broken the law, usually by stealing of some kind or another, and who have been before the courts seem to be very similar to those who have committed the same offences but gone undetected. Therefore, they have similar needs and will very likely respond to identical educative methods. Above all, we should avoid stigmatizing delinquents as criminals or doing anything to support the growth of an anti-social self image. We should also strive to break down peer-group associations which inculcate delinquent attitudes or which enjoin law-breaking activities as part of their way of life. By the same token, approved schools, Borstals and prisons are seen to be as often criminogenic as they are reformatory and correctional.

Sociological and psychological opinions fortunately agree on most of these points. What now remains to be achieved is a general method or series of methods for dealing with the deprived and the delinquent, the unruly and the vulnerable children, which will only in exceptional circumstances involve removal from home and neighbourhood and yet will provide sufficient support against temptation and illicit social influences. The substance of the 1969 Children and Young Persons Bill has much to commend it in this way and when fully implemented should give us many opportunities for dealing constructively and wisely with all children at risk. I am particularly optimistic about the development of intermediate methods which, by involving youth service, education and both voluntary and professional social work, could successfully cope with most of the run-of-the-mill juvenile delinquents and provide them with the necessary amount of guidance and supervision until they have matured sufficiently to have greater self control. There is no need for a great many of these children to be hauled through the courts and submitted to all the legal processes when all they require is someone to take a parental interest in them and something enjoyable to do during their abundant free time. Something like a mixture between attendance centre and tough boys' club might meet their need admirably. At the same time, movements to develop counselling in schools, the closer association of youth work with formal education, growing skill in vocational guidance and other similar developments within the normal environment will mesh most smoothly in with the new child care treatment.

What is abundantly necessary in all kinds of neighbourhoods, and in big towns in particular, is a broad educational social work and welfare movement which would, in the open conditions of everyday living, correspond in quality to the therapeutic milieu as the latter concept has evolved within some hospitals and in residential maladjusted schools.

Unfortunately, as we have demonstrated, there are influences within the social framework which militate against this notion of the caring community and which seek to exploit any and every situation for financial gain. Rogues and confidence men have their counterparts in the business world where sometimes the end, i.e. money-making, increasing sales, etc., justifies the means, i.e. deceitful salesmanship, corruption by advertising, etc. Legalized gambling is another feature in the structure of society which works against true social health. While over all broods the vision of the ubiquitous mass media, pulp literature and the merchandising of sexuality and depravity for profit without the slightest concern for noxious side effects. One does not need to be a puritan to see that much in our national life lends encouragement to delinquent and criminal tendencies and makes the job of rehabilitation much more difficult than it need be. Above all, perhaps, the failure of organized religion and Christian action in the reformatory and after-care field is a positive discouragement to all who work towards social reform and who are actively concerned with the prevention of crime.

In addition, of course, is the constant threat of organized professional crime. Though few in number, the threat from these bandits could assume disastrous proportions. This is most obvious at the moment in trafficking in drugs. Heroin can be smuggled into the country and sold on the organized market at high prices that make it enormously profitable. Meanwhile the deliberate hooking up of youngsters until they are in a dependent condition swells the number of customers and increases the profitability of the trade. One newspaper report stated not long ago that Chinese heroin, which is a particularly impure product, is being smuggled into Britain from Hong Kong at the rate of £80,000 worth per month. Such information, if true, may help us to have a sense of proportion when we are confronted by children said to be beyond parental control or who truant from school or go on shoplifting expeditions and about whom there is so much fuss and to-do in various quarters. The challenge of organized crime and vice is in an entirely different category from what most of us mean when we talk about offenders in social work textbooks and seminars. It involves a deliberate waging of war against the welfare of the community and calls for the most professional and highly organized police work to combat it.

But, to return to the rank and file offenders; research seems to suggest that a more rational approach could pay dividends by saving both cash and manpower. The high success rates with first offenders, even in prison, suggest that most of them, on the grounds of the interchangeability of treatments, could have been dealt with by other ways such as fining, binding over or suspended sentence. What Wilkins and Walker call primary recidivism should be the object of our most subtle attack. It is the potential second offenders who should concern us most and every effort should be made to identify them and rehabilitate them[*] before their criminality becomes chronic and irreversible. Spontaneous or natural recovery is not so likely with these second offenders as it is with first offenders, and those who fail to react favourably to probation should receive specialist treatment, including psychiatric help and group coun-

[*] Here one is referring only to offenders over sixteen or seventeen, not to younger children who may be expected to commit several delinquencies without being stigmatized as recidivists.

selling, within institutions that also provide an adequate degree of privacy and the availability of useful paid work.

It may well be that better prognostic devices and predictive formulae would help us in deciding which are the ones most likely to become primary recidivists. If this proves to be the case, more long term research into the outcomes of various kinds of treatment in relation to specific sorts of offenders will become an urgent necessity.

But one thing is quite obvious: the success of institutionalization depends upon adequate and sustained after-care. This, as I have suggested earlier, requires the setting up of transitional communities which will support ex-detainees for as long as they require such help. These hostels, halfway houses or whatever names are given to them, need to meet the problems of different types of inmates. Some will specialize in helping alcoholics, some in dealing with drug addicts, others will need to specialize in the rehabilitation of emotionally damaged and pseudo-socialized ex-inmates of the new institutions which in time will replace the existing Borstals, while yet others will serve the basically inadequate, rootless older men.

Altogether we are going to need to spend a great deal more time and money on preventive services and on long term rehabilitation in the future if we are to come within measurable distance of being able to cope with and reduce the ever rising tide of crime and delinquency. Will we vote enough money for the purpose? Will we develop the necessary research both into the assessment of penal methods and into a more fundamental understanding of the roots of the problem? Have we sufficient communal generosity to sustain an adequate after-care service? Have we the personal goodness to welcome delinquents back into the community and more particularly into our own homes, workshops and factories without there being any lingering taint of suspiciousness?

Such questions are purely rhetorical. At the same time we must hope that they will receive positive and optimistic answers from the majority of citizens. At the criminological level, one cannot fail to agree with Professor Radzinowicz's rather sombre statement:

(Crime) eludes the coercive reformatory hand, at one time recoiling, but only for a fresh surge forward, at another assuming subtle changes of shape and proportion: sometimes because society itself postulates new offences, or breeds new possibilities of violating its laws, or simply because the art of crime is always developing. But it still abides, a constant symptom in all societies, whatever their racial, national, social, moral and economic condition may happen to be.[3]

But, as a responsible, caring community, we surely cannot leave it there. We owe it to the offenders and non-offenders alike to make an effort to contain and reduce the dimensions of the problem, for, as we well know, sometimes offences are appeals for help, and to refuse to answer would be to abandon some of our less fortunate fellows to a life of continuing misery and social isolation. At the same time we may also have confidence that every improvement in education and welfare, every imaginative policy which makes for greater equality and for a more just sharing of the good things in life, will add its quota to the creation of a healthier, saner and more just society where the seeds of crime will find less nourishment.

# References and further reading

Texts referred to more than once in a chapter are not repeated except when it is necessary for clarity.

CHAPTER I

1. J. B. Mays, *Crime and the Social Structure*, Faber, 1967.
2. This offence is now been recategorized as 'indictable'.
3. T. P. Morris, *The Criminal Area*, Routledge and Kegan Paul, 1957.
4. H. Mannheim, *Comparative Criminology*, Routledge and Kegan Paul, 1965.
5. C. H. Rolph, *Common Sense about Crime and Punishment*, Gollancz, 1961.
6. J. H. Bagot, *Juvenile Delinquency*, Cape, 1941, p. 23.
7. H. Silcock, *The Increase in Crimes of Theft, 1938–47*, Liverpool University Press, 1949.
8. J. Trenaman, *Out of Step*, Methuen, 1952, Appendix A.
9. T. Ferguson, *The Young Delinquent in his Social Setting*, Oxford, 1952; J. B. Mays, *Growing Up in the City*, Liverpool University Press, 1954; J. P. Martin, *Offenders As Employees*, Cambridge, 1962; R. G. Andry, *Delinquency and Parental Pathology*, Methuen, 1960; P. Willmott, *Adolescent Boys of East London*, Routledge and Kegan Paul, 1966; D. H. Hargreaves, *Social Relations in a Secondary School*, Routledge and Kegan Paul, 1967; Lynn McDonald, *Social Class and Delinquency*, Faber, 1969.
10. See James Short Jnr and I. Nye, 'Reported Behaviour as a Criterion of Deviant Behaviour', *The Sociology of Crime and Delinquency*, eds. Wolfgang, Savitz and Johnston, Wiley, 1962, pp. 44–49.
11. Lee Robins, *Deviant Children Grown Up*, Williams and Wilkins, Baltimore, 1966.

12. See John Mack, 'Police Juvenile Liaison Schemes', *Brit. J. Crim.* 3, 1963, 361–375, and J. B. Mays, 'The Liverpool Police Liaison Officer Scheme', *Sociological Review Monograph No. 9, Sociological Studies in the British Penal Services*, Keele, 1965, 185–209.

13. D. West, *Who Becomes Delinquent?*, Heinemann, 1973.

14. L. Radzinowicz, ed. *Sexual Offenders*, Macmillan, 1957.

*Further reading:*
Howard Jones, *Crime in a Changing Society*, Penguin Books, 1965.

CHAPTER 2

1. C. H. Rolph, *Common Sense about Crime and Punishment*.

2. F. H. McClintock and E. Gibson, *Robbery in London*, Macmillan, 1961.

3. H. Avison, 'The New Pattern of Crime', *New Society*, 8th September 1966.

4. *15–18*, Report of the Crowther Committee, H.M.S.O., 1959.

5. B. Wootton, *Crime and the Criminal Law*, Stevens, 1963.

6. G. Sykes, *Crime and Society*, Random House, 1956.

7. E. H. Sutherland, *Principles of Criminology*, 5th edn., ed. D. Cressey, Lippincott, New York, 1955.

8. Reproduced from L. Wilkins, 'What is Crime?', *New Society*, 18th July 1963.

9. Martin Silverman, *Aspects of Drug Addiction*, Royal London Prisoners' Aid Society, London, 1967.

*Further reading:*
F. H. McClintock, H. Avison, *Crime in England and Wales*, Heinemann, 1968.

CHAPTER 3

1. B. Wootton, 'Are There Causes of Crime?', *The Observer*, 18 January 1958.

2. E. H. Sutherland, *White Collar Crime*, Foreword by D. Cressey, Holt, Rinehart and Winston, New York, 1961.

3. Jackson Toby, 'Criminal Motivation', *Brit. J. Crim.* 2, 1962, pp. 317–336.
4. W. F. Roper, 'A Survey of Wakefield Prison, 1948–49', *Brit. J. Delinq.* 1, 1950, pp. 15–28.
5. Emile Durkheim, *The Rules of the Sociological Method*, Free Press, Illinois, 1939.
6. A. Comfort, *Authority and Delinquency in the Modern State*, Routledge and Kegan Paul, 1950.
7. E. Durkheim, *The Division of Labour in Society*, Free Press, 1947.
8. S. Glueck, 'Theory and Fact in Criminology', *Brit. J. Delinq.* 7, 1956, pp. 92–109.
9. E. Glover, *The Roots of Crime*, Imago, London, 1960.
10. E. Durkheim, *Suicide*, ed. G. Simpson, Routledge and Kegan Paul, 1952.
11. D. Taft, *Criminology*, Macmi'lan, New York, 1956.
12. W. F. Whyte, *Streetcorner Society*, University of Chicago Press, 1943.
13. M. Clinard, *The Black Market*, Rinehart, New York, 1952.
14. J. B. Mays, *Crime and the Social Structure*.
15. E. Sutherland, *White Collar Crime*.
16. D. Cressey, *Delinquency, Crime and Differential Association*, Nijhoff, The Hague, 1964.
17. L. Blom-Cooper, 'White Collar Crime', *Frontiers of Criminology*, Pergamon, London, 1967, p. 44.
18. L. Blom-Cooper, *ibid*.
19. G. E. Levens, '101 White Collar Criminals', *New Society*, 26 March 1964.
20. D. Cressey, *ibid*.
21. L. T. Wilkins, *Social Deviance*, Tavistock, London, 1964.

22. Robert K. Merton, *Social Theory and Social Structure*, Revised ed., The Free Press, Illinois, 1957.

23. See D. Szabo, 'The socio-cultural approach to the aetiology of delinquent behaviour', *Modern Methods in Criminology, International Social Science Journal*, Vol. XVIII, 2, Unesco, 1966, p. 187.

*Further reading:*

T. C. N. Gibbens and R. H. Ahrenfeldt, *Cultural Factors in Delinquency*, Tavistock, London, 1966.

Marshall B. Clinard, *Sociology of Deviant Behaviour*, Revised ed., Holt, Rinehart and Winston, New York, 1965.

CHAPTER 4

1. H. Mannheim, *Comparative Criminology*.

2. T. P. Morris, *The Criminal Area*.

3. Lynn McDonald, *Social Class and Delinquency*.

4. E. Vaz, *Middle-Class Juvenile Delinquency*, Harper and Row, New York, 1967.

5. B. Markus, 'A Dimensional Study of a Prison Population', *Brit. J. Crimin.* 1, 1960, pp. 130–153.

6. J. B. Mays, 'Crime and the Urban Pattern', *The Sociological Review*, 16, No. 2, July 1968, p. 253.

7. A. Cohen, *Delinquent Boys, The Culture of the Gang*, Routledge and Kegan Paul, 1956.

8. P. Laurie, *Teenage Revolution*, Blond, London, 1965.

9. C. Shaw and H. McKay, *Juvenile Delinquency in Urban Areas*, University of Chicago Press, 1942.

10. W. B. Miller, 'Lower Class Culture as a Generating Milieu of Gang Delinquency', *The Sociology of Crime and Delinquency*, eds. Wolfgang, Savitz and Johnston, pp. 267–276.

11. R. Cloward and L. Ohlin, *Delinquency and Opportunity*, Routledge and Kegan Paul, 1961.

# REFERENCES AND FURTHER READING

12. I. Spergel, *Racketville, Slumtown and Haulberg*, Chicago University Press, 1964.
13. M. Gold, *Status Forces in Delinquent Boys*, Ann Arbor, Michigan, 1963.
14. James F. Short and F. L. Strodtbeck, *Group Process in Gang Delinquency*, University of Chicago Press, 1965.
15. D. Matza, *Delinquency and Drift*, Wiley, New York, 1964.
16. L. Yablonsky, *The Violent Gang*, Macmillan, New York, 1962: Penguin Books, London, 1967.
17. Matza, *ibid*.
18. Cyril Burt, *The Young Delinquent*, University of London Press, 1925.
19. J. B. Mays, *Growing Up in The City*.
20. *The Social Background of Delinquency*, University of Nottingham for private circulation only, 1954.
21. C. Bagley, 'Juvenile Delinquency in Exeter: An Ecological and Comparative Study', *Urban Studies*, 2, No. 1, 1965, pp. 33–50.
22. Morris, *op. cit.*
23. P. Willmott, *Adolescent Boys of East London*.
24. D. Downes, *The Delinquent Solution*, Routledge and Kegan Paul, 1966.
25. P. Elton Mayo, *The Making of a Criminal*, Weidenfeld and Nicolson, 1969.
26. J. A. Mack, 'Full-time Miscreants, Delinquent Neighbourhoods and Criminal Networks,' *British Journal of Sociology*, vol. 15, 1964.
27. H. Parker, *View from the Boys,* David and Charles, 1974.

*Further reading:*

F. Thrasher, *The Gang*, Abridged with an introduction by James F. Short, Jnr., University of Chicago Press, 1963.

D. J. West, *Present Conduct and Future Delinquency*, Heinemann, 1969.

CHAPTER 5

1. Lee Robins, *Deviant Children Growing Up*.
2. B. Wootton, *Social Science and Social Pathology*, Allen and Unwin, 1959.

3. F. Ivan Nye, *Family Relationships and Delinquent Behaviour*, New York, Wiley, 1958.

4. S. Yudkin and A. Holme, *Working Mothers and Their Children*, Michael Joseph, 1963.

5. S. and E. Glueck, *Unravelling Juvenile Delinquency*, New York, 1950.

6. R. G. Andry, *Delinquency and Parental Pathology*.

7. Nye, *ibid*.

8. H. Wilson, *Delinquency and Child Neglect*, Allen and Unwin, 1962.

9. Cyril Burt, *The Causes and Treatment of Backwardness*, University of London Press, 1952.

10. J. Webb, 'The Sociology of a School', *Brit. J. Sociology*, 13, No. 3, 1962, pp. 264–270.

11. A. Clegg and B. Megson, *Children in Distress*, Penguin Books, 1968.

12. D. Hargreaves, *Social Relations in a Secondary School*.

13. M. Power, R. Benn and J. N. Morris, 'Neighbourhood, School and Juveniles Before The Courts', *British Journal of Criminology*, 12, No. 2, 1972.

14. D. Downes, *The Delinquent Solution*.

15. Tony Parker, *The Unknown Citizen*, Hutchinson, 1965: Penguin Books, 1966.

*Further reading:*

G. Trasler, *The Meaning of Criminality*, Routledge and Kegan Paul, 1962.

S. and E. Glueck, *Family Environment and Delinquency*, Routledge and Kegan Paul, 1962.

CHAPTER 6

1. *Guardian*, 15 May 1969.

2. W. Moberley, *The Ethics of Punishment*, Faber, 1968.

3. N. Walker, *Crime and Punishment in Britain*, Edinburgh, 1965, p. 131.

4. L. Wilkins, *Social Deviance*, p. 74.
5. Jackson Toby, 'Criminal Motivation'.
6. I. Croft and T. Grygier, 'Social Relationships of Truants and Juvenile Delinquents', *Human Relations*, 9, 1956, pp. 439–466.
7. A. V. Cicourel, *The Social Organisation of Juvenile Justice*, Wiley, 1968.
8. S. Cohen, *Folk Devils and Moral Panics*, MacGibbon and Kee, 1972.

*Further reading:*

Lord Devlin, *The Enforcement of Morals*, Oxford, 1965.

H. L. A. Hart, *Law, Liberty and Morals*, Oxford, 1963.

Margery Fry, *Arms of the Law*, Gollancz, 1951.

CHAPTER 7

1. F. H. McClintock, *Attendance Centres*, Macmillan, 1961.
2. *The Results of Probation*, Macmillan, 1958.
3. L. T. Wilkins, 'A Small Comparative Study of the Results of Probation', *Brit. J. Delinq.* 8, 1958, pp. 201–09.
4. M. Davies, *Probationers in their Social Environment*, Home Office Research Unit Report, H.M.S.O., 1969.
5. W. David Wills, *Throw Away Thy Rod*, Gollancz, 1960.
6. M. Burn, *Mr. Lyward's Answer*, Hamish Hamilton, 1956.
7. O. Shaw, *Maladjusted Boys*, Allen and Unwin, 1965.
8. F. G. Llenhoff, *Exceptional Children*, Allen and Unwin, 1960.
9. D. Wills, *Homer Lane: A Biography*, Allen and Unwin, 1964.
10. O. Gill, *Whitegate, An Approved School in Transition*, Liverpool University Press, 1974.
11. White Paper, *Statistics Relating to Approved Schools, Remand Homes, and Attendance Centres in England and Wales, for the year 1965*, H.M.S.O.

12. E. Field, 'Research Into Detention Centres', *Brit. J. Crimin.* 9, 1969, pp. 62–71.
13. *Sunday Telegraph*, 21 July 1968.
14. T. C. N. Gibbens and J. Prince, 'The Results of Borstal Training', *Sociological Review Monograph No. 9. Sociological Studies in the British Penal Services*, pp. 227–236.
15. R. G. Hood, *Homeless Borstal Boys*, Occasional Papers on Social Administration, No. 18, London, 1966.
16. R. Cockett, 'Borstal Training: A Follow-up Study', *Brit. J. Crimin.* 7, 1967, pp. 150–183.
17. 'Magistrate at the Test Bench', *Guardian*, 24 July 1969.
18. H. Klare, *Anatomy of Prison*, Hutchinson, 1960, p. 28.
19. D. Clemmer, 'Prisonization', *The Sociology of Punishment and Correction*, eds. Johnston, Savitz and Wolfgang, Wiley, 1962, pp. 148–151.
20. G. Sykes, *The Society of Captives*, Princeton, 1958.
21. T. P. and P. Morris, *Pentonville*, Routledge and Kegan Paul, 1963.
22. I. Horobin, 'What Prison Taught Me', The *Observer*, 10 October 1965.
23. Cmnd. 3175, December 1966. H.M.S.O.
24. *The Regime for Long-Term Prisoners in Conditions of Maximum Security*, first report of the Advisory Council on the Penal System, 1968.

*Further reading:*

J. King, *The Probation Service*, Butterworth, 1964.

A. G. Rose, *Schools for Young Offenders*, Tavistock, 1967.

W. E. Cavanagh, *The Child and the Court*, Gollancz, 1959.

J. Watson, *The Child and the Magistrate*, Cape, 1965.

L. Fox, *The English Prison and Borstal Systems*, Routledge and Kegan Paul, 1952.

D. M. Lowson, *City Lads in Borstal*, Liverpool University Press, 1970.

CHAPTER 8

1. J. B. Mays, 'The Liverpool Police Liaison Officer Scheme', *Sociological Review Monograph, No. 9: Sociological Studies in The British Penal Services*, 1965, pp. 185–200.

2. H. Mannheim and L. Wilkins, *Prediction Methods in Relation to Borstal Training*, H.M.S.O., 1955.
3. S. and E. Glueck, *Predicting Delinquency and Crime*, Harvard University Press, 1960.
4. D. H. Stott, 'The Prediction of Delinquency from Non-Delinquent Behaviour', *Brit. J. Delinq.* 10, 1960, pp. 202–210.
5. L. Ohlin, 'Predicting Parole Behaviour', *The Sociology of Punishment and Correction*, eds. Johnston, Savitz and Wolfgang, Wiley, 1962, pp. 282–291.
6. N. Fenton, *An Introduction to Group Counselling in State Correctional Services*, New York, 1958.
7. *Group Work in Prisons and Borstals, 1962–6*, Home Office Prison Department, 1966.
8. *Ibid.*
9. *Ibid.*
10. M. Turner, *Safe Lodging*, Hutchinson, 1961.
11. D. Miller, *Growth to Freedom*, Tavistock, 1964.
12. Report on Children and Young Persons (Scotland), 1964 Cmnd. 2306.
13. Cmnd. 2742, 1965.
14. Cmnd. 3601, 1968.

*Further reading:*

T. Sellin and M. Wolfgang, *The Measurement of Delinquency*, Wiley, New York, 1964.

R. Schwitzgebel, *Street-Corner Research*, Harvard University Press, 1964.

CHAPTER 9

1. Part of this section has already been printed in the *Sociological Review*, 16, No. 2, 1968, pp. 250–253.

2. H. M. Shulman, *Juvenile Delinquency in American Society*, Harper, 1961, and B. Lander, *Towards an Understanding of Juvenile Delinquency*, Columbia University Press, 1954.

3. L. Radzinowicz, *In Search of Criminology*, Heinemann, 1961.

*Further reading:*

M. Wolfgang (ed.) *Crime and Culture: Essays in Honor of Thorsten Sellin*, Wiley, 1968.

M. Ancel, *Social Defence*, Routledge and Kegan Paul, 1965.

*Suggested Additional Reading:*

I. Taylor, P. Walton and J. Young, *The New Criminology*, Routledge and Kegan Paul, 1973.

P. Rock, *Deviant Behaviour*, Hutchinson, 1973.

R. Hood and R. Sparks, *Key Issues in Criminology*, Weidenfeld and Nicolson, 1970.

E. Rubington and M. S. Weinberg, *Deviance: The Interactionist Perspective*, Macmillan, New York, 1968.

J. B. Mays, *Juvenile Delinquency, The Family and The Social Group*, Longman, 1972.

J. B. Mays, *The Social Treatment of Young Offenders*, Longman, 1975.

James Patrick, *A Glasgow Gang Observed*, Eyre Methuen, 1973.

# Criminal statistics, graphs and tables

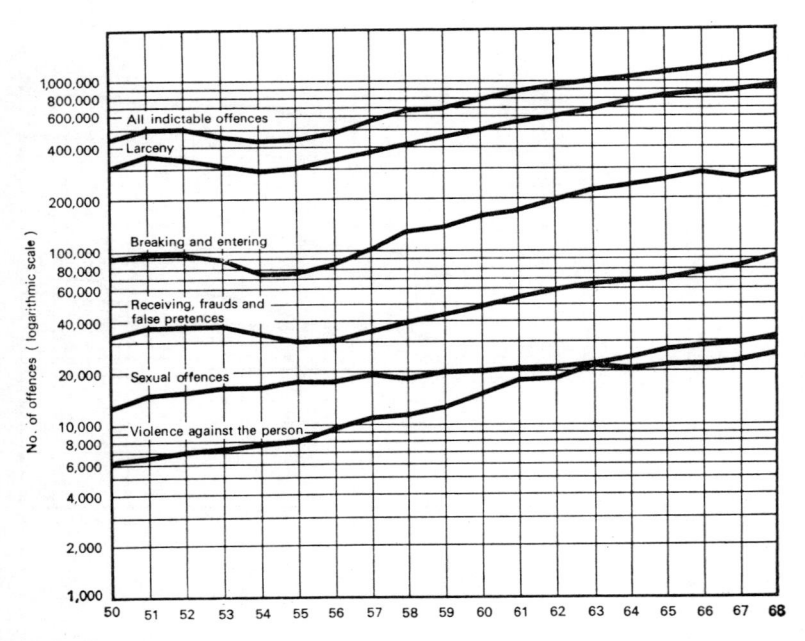

FIGURE 4(a)
*Indictable offences known to the police 1950-1968.*

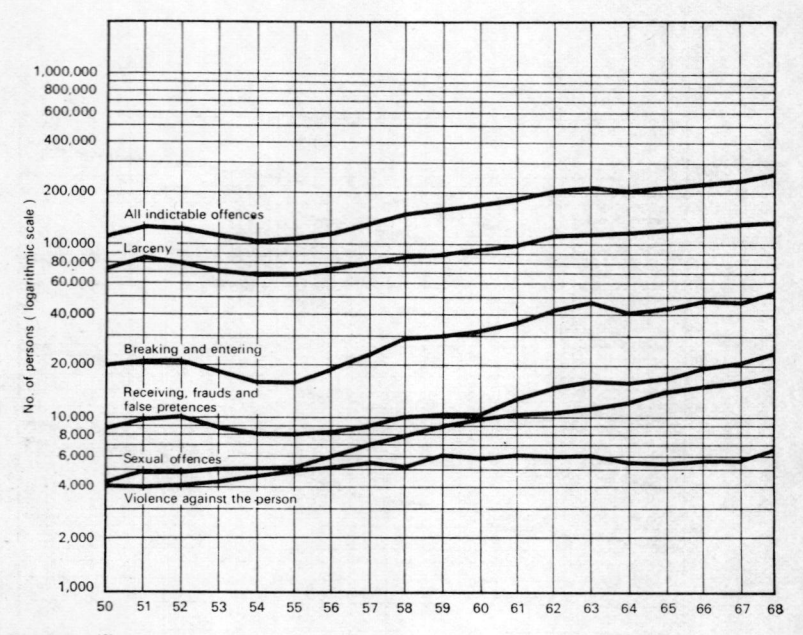

FIGURE 4(*b*)
*Persons found guilty of indictable offences 1950-1968.*

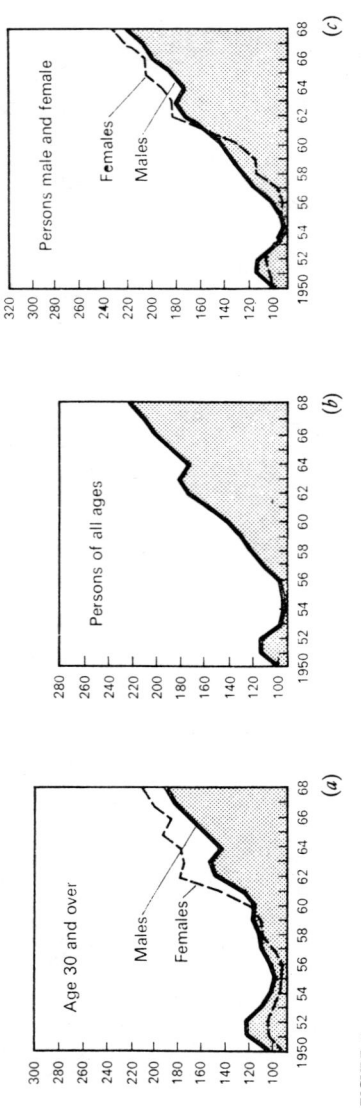

**FIGURE 5**
*Indictable Offences 1950–1968. Variations related to 1950—100 persons found guilty at all courts.*

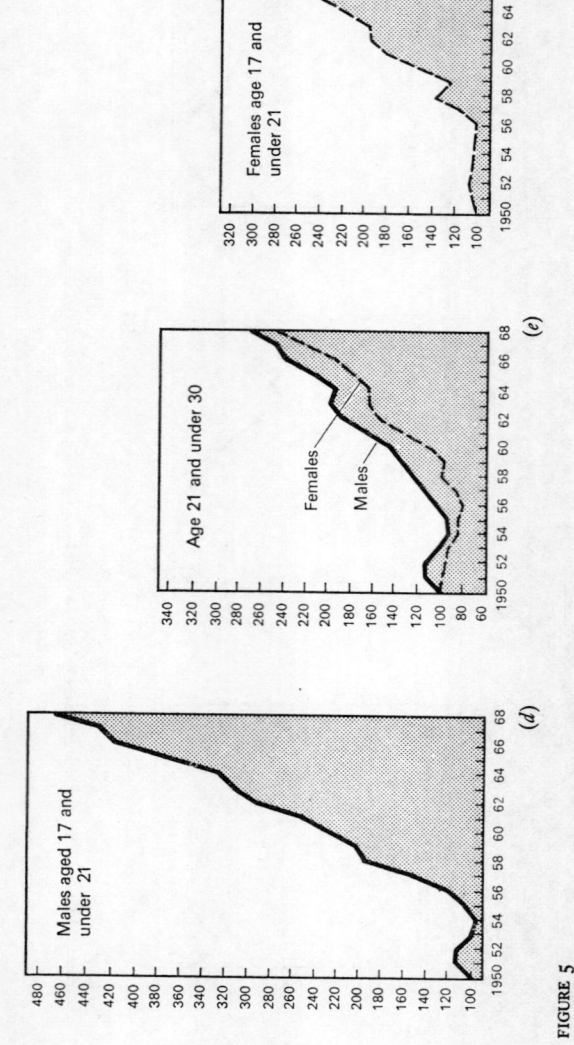

FIGURE 5
*Indictable offences 1950–1968—continued. Variations related to 1950—100 persons found guilty at all courts.*

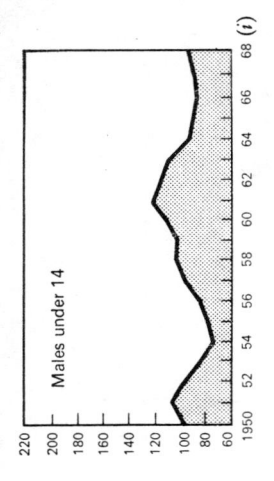

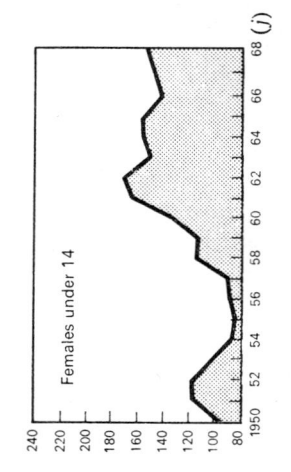

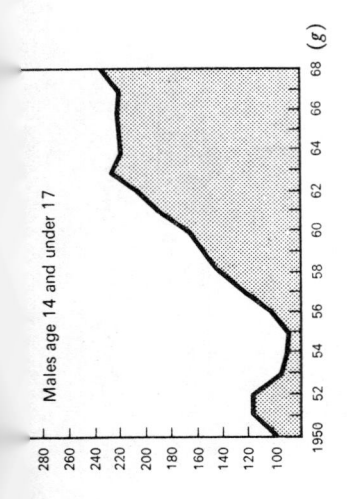

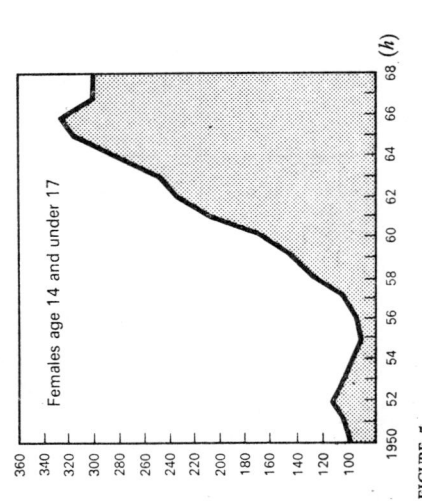

FIGURE 5
*Indictable offences 1950–1968—continued. Variations related to 1950—100 persons found guilty at all courts.*

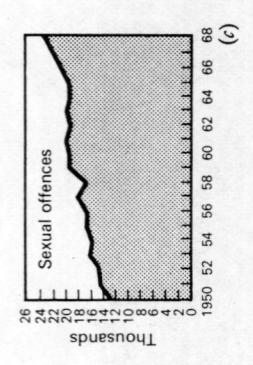

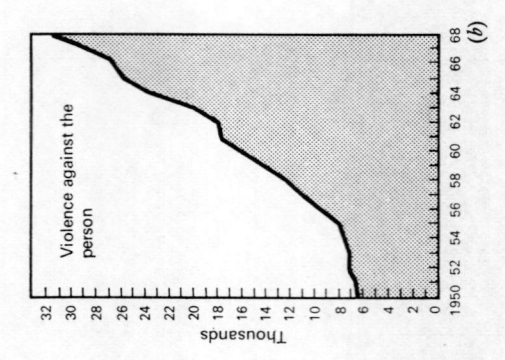

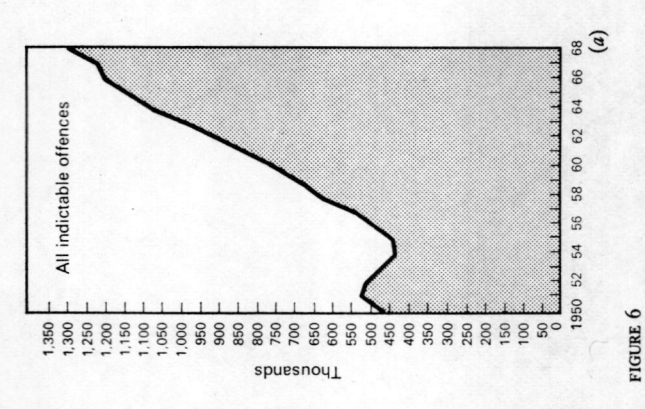

FIGURE 6
*Indictable offences known to the police 1950-1968.*

FIGURE 6
*Indictable offences known to the police 1950–1968—continued.*

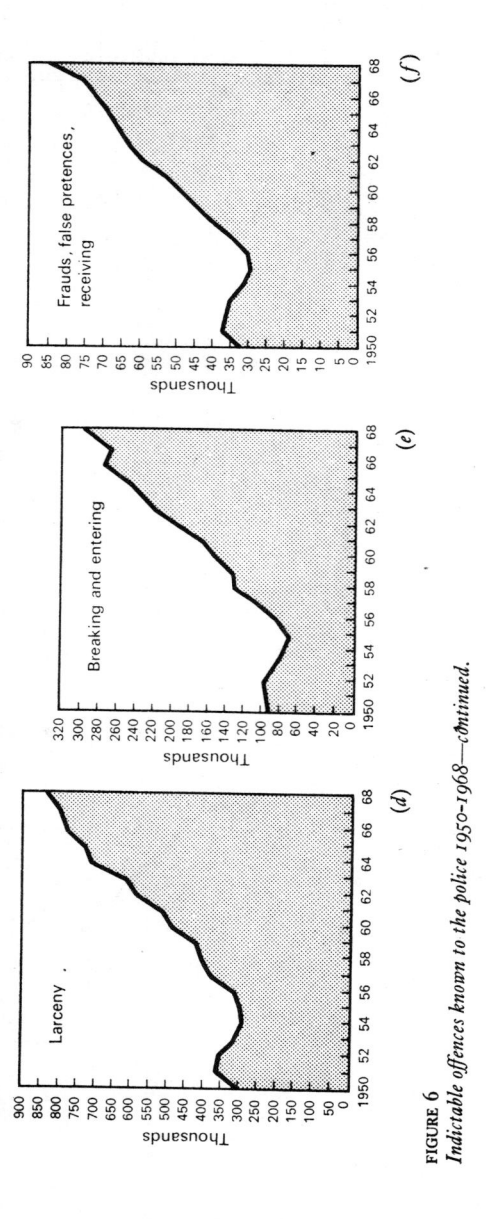

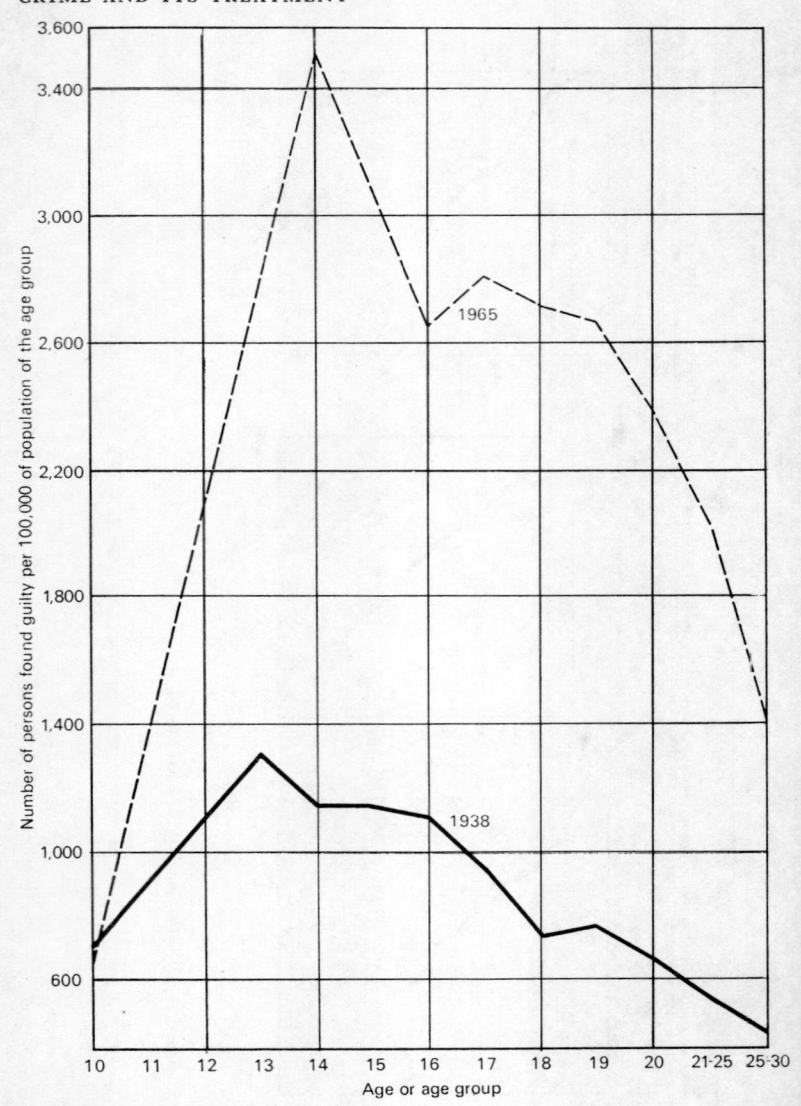

FIGURE 7
*Number of males of different ages found guilty of indictable offences: 1938 and 1965.*

# CRIMINAL STATISTICS, GRAPHS AND TABLES

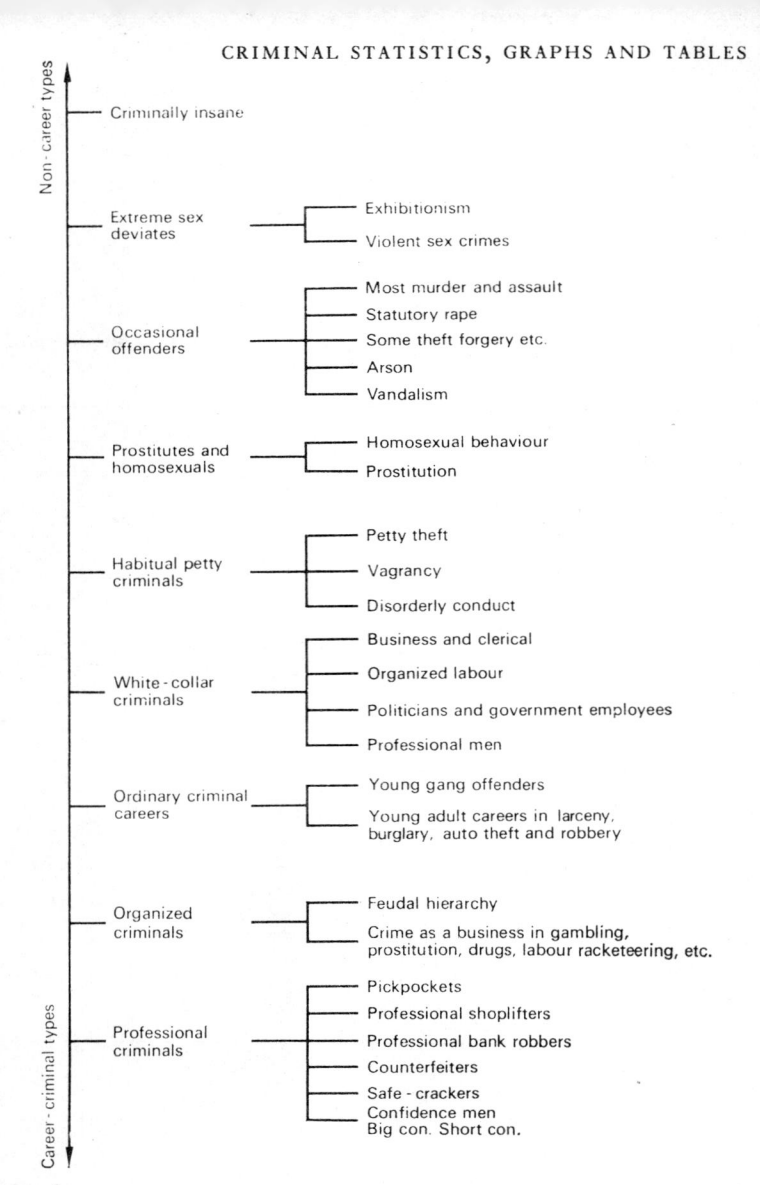

Non-career types
- Criminally insane
- Extreme sex deviates
  - Exhibitionism
  - Violent sex crimes
- Occasional offenders
  - Most murder and assault
  - Statutory rape
  - Some theft forgery etc.
  - Arson
  - Vandalism
- Prostitutes and homosexuals
  - Homosexual behaviour
  - Prostitution

Career-criminal types
- Habitual petty criminals
  - Petty theft
  - Vagrancy
  - Disorderly conduct
- White-collar criminals
  - Business and clerical
  - Organized labour
  - Politicians and government employees
  - Professional men
- Ordinary criminal careers
  - Young gang offenders
  - Young adult careers in larceny, burglary, auto theft and robbery
- Organized criminals
  - Feudal hierarchy
  - Crime as a business in gambling, prostitution, drugs, labour racketeering, etc.
- Professional criminals
  - Pickpockets
  - Professional shoplifters
  - Professional bank robbers
  - Counterfeiters
  - Safe-crackers
  - Confidence men
  - Big con. Short con.

**FIGURE 8**
*Selected types of delinquent and criminal behaviour (Clinard, 1963).*

## Table 4

*Numbers of persons found guilty of offences of drunkenness (Home Office classes 140 and 141)*

| AGE AND SEX | | 1955 | 1959 | 1963 | 1965 |
|---|---|---|---|---|---|
| Up to 14 | Male | — | 2 | 1 | 6 |
| | Female | — | — | — | — |
| 14–16 | Male | 184 | 290 | 483 | 541 |
| | Female | 21 | 34 | 53 | 58 |
| 17–20 | Male | 3688 | 5394 | 7570 | 8032 |
| | Female | 205 | 228 | 247 | 202 |
| 21 and over | Male | 43,667 | 52,442 | 66,887 | 56,670 |
| | Female | 4261 | 4145 | 4357 | 3496 |

| | | Rate 1955 = 100 | | |
|---|---|---|---|---|
| AGE AND SEX | | 1959 | 1963 | 1965 |
| Up to 14 | Male | — | — | — |
| | Female | — | — | — |
| 14–16 | Male | 157·6 | 262·5 | 294·0 |
| | Female | 161·9 | 252·4 | 276·2 |
| 17–20 | Male | 146·3 | 205·3 | 217·8 |
| | Female | 111·2 | 120·5 | 98·5 |
| 21 and over | Male | 120·1 | 153·2 | 129·8 |
| | Female | 97·3 | 102·3 | 82·0 |

# Index

adolescence and crime, 16, 17, 22, 23, 47, 49, 55, 59
after care, 95, 99, 103, 104, 108, 115–16, 131, 147
*A Glasgow Gang Observed*, 68
Andry, R. J., 72
*anomia*, 42
*anomie*, 31, 40–3, 50, 139, 140, 141
approved schools, 85, 86, 93, 98–101, 104, 106, 107, 143
attendance centres, 94–5, 145
Avison, Howard, 15, 21, 22

'Black Market', 8, 35
Booth, Charles, 62
Borstal, 83, 84, 85, 93, 103, 104–6, 110, 112, 113, 115, 116, 120, 123, 124, 125, 126, 144, 147
Brain Committee, 23
Bristol Social Adjustment Guide, 121
Buckinghamshire, 21
Burgess, E., 120, 140
Burt, Sir Cyril, 62, 74

Cambridge Institute of Criminology, 14, 95, 96
Capone, Al, 29
Chicago, 49–52, 54, 59, 143
child guidance clinics, 70
Children Act 1908, 83
Children Act 1933, 7
Children Act 1963, 83

Children and Young Persons Act 1969, 83, 89, 93, 98, 119, 132, 136, 137
*Children in Trouble*, 122, 134, 135
*The Child, the Family, and the Young Offender*, 134
Cicourel, A., 91
classification of offenders, 113–15
Clegg, Sir Alec, 75
Clemmer, D., 111
Clinard, Marshall, 32, 35
Cloward, R., 22, 55, 56, 57, 59, 60, 62, 67, 140
Cockett, Dr, 105
Cohen, A., 48, 53, 54, 58, 59, 60, 61, 62, 64, 67, 75, 140
Cohen, S., 91
Comfort, Dr. Alex, 29
community homes, 88, 93, 98–101, 137
Community Service Orders, 86, 131–2
conditional discharge, 129
corrective training, 109
courts (juvenile), 93, 94, 104
Court Lees School, 85, 100
Cressey, Donald, 33, 39
crime,
 and differential roles, 18, 19
 and gambling, 145
 and heredity, 25
 'hidden', 8–12, 50, 63

169

# INDEX

and immaturity, 27-8
juvenile, 4, 8, 11, 12, 16, 18, 22, 45, 49, 57, 62-9, 70-8, 90, 93-107, 125-6, 132-7
and learning, 26-8
and maturation, 16, 17, 30
and morality, 4, 5, 6, 21, 29, 36, 47, 145
and normality, 11, 28, 29, 30, 31, 91
and opportunity, 19-22, 36, 56
prevention, 89
and school-leaving age, 17
and schools, 74-6, 90
and self-images, 34, 58, 90, 111, 144
self-reported, 10, 11
and sex, 16-19
and social class, 44-69, 138-9, 141, 142
and socialization, 70-8
statistics, 2, 6, 7, 8, 9, 11, 13, 14, 44, 138-9, 141, 142
subcultural, 28, 29, 52, 53, 56-7, 61-9, 139-41
'white-collar', 4, 12, 26, 32-7, 46, 77, 141
*see also* offences
Criminal Justice Act 1948, 84, 87, 94, 102
Criminal Justice Act 1967, 126
Criminal Justice Bill 1966, 109
Criminal Justice Act 1972, 128, 130-2
criminogenic society, 4, 31, 32, 35, 37, 42, 91-2, 139, 143, 145
Croft, I. (and Grygier, T.), 90-1

Davies, M., 98

Day Training Centres, 86, 130-1, 132
delinquency, *see* crime
delinquency areas, 9, 74, 76, 140, 141
delinquency and the family, 15, 48, 58, 63, 70, 71, 72, 73, 74, 139
detention centres, 84, 93, 102-4, 107, 110, 112, 137
deterrence, 82-3
'differential association', theory of, 38-9
discharge, 94
discipline, 62, 75, 82, 102
Downes, David, 67-8, 76
drugs, (drug addiction), 23, 47, 57, 130, 146, 147
drunkenness, 22, 23
Du Cane, 82
Durkheim, E., 29, 30, 31, 32, 38, 40, 53

Emmett, B. P., 9
Exeter, 16

Fenton, Dr, 123
Field, Elizabeth, 102
fines, 43, 108
Fry, Margery, 86

gangs, 51, 53, 54, 55, 56-7, 60
Gibbens, T. C. N., 105
Gill, Owen, 101
Glaser, D., 40
Glover, Edward, 30
Glueck, Sheldon and Eleanor, 25, 30, 72, 89, 120, 121
Gold, M., 57-8
group counselling, 123-5

# INDEX

group work in prisons and Borstals, 123–5

half-way houses, 125–6, 147
Hargreaves, David, 75–6
Holloway Prison, 18, 110
Home Office Research Unit, 97
homicide, 8, 15, 79
Hood, Dr, 105
hostels, 125–6, 147
Howard League for Penal Reform, 5, 81, 130

immigrants, 50, 57
Ingleby Committee Report, 118
'intermediate treatment of offenders', 86, 136–7, 144

Juvenile liaison officers, 117–19

Kilbrandon Committee, 133
Kilbrandon, Lord, 133
Klare, Hugh, 111

Lane, Homer, 101
Levens, G. E., 36
Llenhoff, F. G., 100
Liverpool, 45, 63, 65, 69, 117, 118, 130
Lombroso, 25
Longford, Lord, 134
Lyward, George, 100

Mack, John, 69
McClintock, F., 95
McDonald, Dr L., 45
McKay, Henry, 49–52, 140
magistrates, 91, 100, 108
*mala in se*, 1, 3
*mala prohibita*, 1
Mannheim, Dr H., 4, 8, 44, 52, 120, 122

Marcus, B., 47
Matza, David, 46, 59, 61–2
Mayo, Mrs E., 68–9
*mens rea*, 1
Merseyside, *see* Liverpool
Merton, Robert K., 40, 53, 55
Miller, Derek, 126
Miller, W. B., 54, 55, 58, 59, 66, 74, 140
Misuse of Drugs Act, 1971, 23
Moberley, Sir W., 81
Mods and Rockers, 91
Moors Murder Case, 115
Morris, T. P., 2, 44, 66, 74, 111, 140
Mountbatten Report, 85, 113–14, 125

N.A.C.R.O., 115
'neutralization techniques', 61
Norman House, 125
Northways, 126
Nye, Ivan, 10, 72

offences,
  'benign', 1, 4, 143
  indictable, 2, 13, 14, 16, 22
  'malignant', 1, 4, 143
  non-indictable, 2, 13, 14
  peak-age, 1, 16–18
  property, 9, 11, 12, 13, 14, 20
  sexual, 5, 7, 8, 11, 12, 47–8, 102
  violent, 14, 15, 80
offenders, habitual, *see*
  recidivists, 77, 78, 84
  typology of, 25, 47, 77
Ohlin, Lloyd, 22, 55, 56, 57, 59, 60, 62, 67, 122, 140

# INDEX

Park, R. E., 49
Parker, Howard, 69
Parker, Tony, 77
parole, 84, 116, 122, 126–9
Parsons, Talcott, 48
Paterson, Alexander, 84
Patrick, J., 68
police,
   efficiency of, 6, 82
   discretion, 8
   cautions, 8
   juvenile liaison officers, 11, 117–19
   public relations, 14
prediction, 147
Preventive detention, 87, 109
prison, 106–7, 108–11, 144
   rules, 111
   security, 85, 113–14
   success rates, 110
   welfare officers, 116
prisonization, 111–12
probation, 84, 91, 95–8, 107, 108, 115, 116, 128, 129, 131, 135, 143
probation hostels, 107
problem families, 73–4, 140
professional crime, 21, 22, 77–8, 145–6
Profumo affair, 36
psychiatry and crime, 29–30, 143, 145–6

Radby, 64–5
Radzinowicz, Leon, 12, 114, 147
recidivism (primary), 116, 146, 147
recidivists, 22, 77, 84, 109, 130, 144
relative deprivation and crime, (*see also* anomie), 3, 42
remand homes, 107

restitution, 86
robberies, 21, 22
*Robbery in London*, 14
Robins, Dr L., 10, 11, 70, 71
Rolph, C. H., 7, 14
Rolling Stones, 49
Roper, Dr W. F., 27
Ruggles-Brise, E., 84

Seebohm Committee Report, 95
Shaw, Clifford, 49–52, 140
Shaw, Otto, 100
Sheldon, W. H., 25
Sherman Anti-Trust Law, 33
shoplifters, 11, 20
Short, James, 10, 59
Silcock, H., 9
social defence, 87–8
Social Medicine Research Unit, 76
Social Work (Scotland) Bill, 1968, 133
Socrates, 29
Sprott, W. J. H., 64, 140
Srole, L., 42
Stott, Dr D. H., 89, 121
Strodtbeck, S., 59–60
suicide, 5, 7, 31
Supervision Orders, 98, 136
suspended sentences, 98, 129–30
Sutherland, Edwin, 19, 25, 26, 32–3, 38–40, 50, 55
Sykes, Gresham, 19, 111
Szabo, 42

Taft, Donald, 31, 32
Tarde, G., 25
Thrasher, F., 51, 54, 74
Thomas, W. I., 2
Toby, Jackson, 26

Trenaman, J., 9
Trenchard, Lord, 7
Turner, Mervyn, 126

United States of America, 13, 19, 26, 31, 39, 40, 46, 49, 56, 82, 114

Vaz, E., 46
Veblen, T., 32

Wakefield Prison, 47, 113
Walker, N., 146
Webb, John, 74

West, Dr D. J., 12
'white collar' offences/offenders *see* crime
Whyte, W. F., 32
Wilkins, Leslie, 20, 40, 90, 97, 120, 122, 146
Willmott, P., 66–7
Wills, David, 100
Wilson, Harriet, 73, 140
Wootton, Barbara, 18, 25, 72
Wootton Report, 131

Yablonsky, L., 60
Yudkin, S., and Holme, A., 72